Getting Ahead in the Music Business

ZADOC MUSIC BUSINESS SERIES

available

Promoting Rock Concerts
     by Howard Stein with Ronald Zalkind
Getting Ahead in the Music Business
     by Ronald Zalkind

in preparation

Producing Hit Records
Understanding Music Business Contracts, 2 vols.
Financial Planning for Entrepreneurs in the Arts
Writing Hit Songs
The Contemporary Music Almanac

Getting Ahead in the Music Business

by RONALD ZALKIND

SCHIRMER BOOKS
A Division of Macmillan Publishing Co., Inc.
NEW YORK

Collier Macmillan Publishers
LONDON

Grateful appreciation is expressed to Stanley Garrett, for his long-time contribution of legal services, and to Bob Reno, president of Midland International Records, and Bruce Lundvall, president of CBS Records, whose interest in music business education has permitted this work to evolve. And special thanks to Marian Smith, a former student now working in the international department of RCA Records, for reading the manuscript and miscellaneous contributions to Zadoc over the years. — RZ

A Zadoc Book

Zadoc® is a registered trademark protected by law.

Copyright© 1979 by Ronald Zalkind

SCHIRMER BOOKS
A Division of Macmillan Publishing Co., Inc.
866 Third Avenue, New York, N.Y.   10022

Collier Macmillan Canada, Ltd.

Library of Congress Catalog Card Number: 79-7366

Printed in the United States of America

printing number

1   2   3   4   5   6   7   8   9   10

Library of Congress Cataloging in Publication Data

Zalkind, Ronald.
    Getting ahead in the music business.

    "A Zadoc book."
    1. Music trade—United States.   2. Music—Economic aspects.   3. Music as a profession.   I. Title.
ML3790.Z34   338.4'7'78   79-7366
ISBN 0-02-872990-0
ISBN 0-02-873000-3pbk.

For the Yeadonites:

*Barbara, Robbie, Grandmother,
and my parents*

Contents

Part 5. ARTIST AND SONGWRITER NEEDS

Preface

If you want a career in the music business (and in today's world you're probably in the minority if you haven't dreamed of becoming a superstar), this book is meant for you. It's not a book about the music business per se, or about music business contracts, or record promotion, or music merchandising, or any of dozens of other textbook subjects. It's a book about how to get ahead in the music business: how to take what you have to the marketplace, make money, and, I hope, have a successful career.

I'm not going to pretend that a uniform success formula exists, or that I have all the answers. But I do think it's time that someone with an insider's understanding of the business got to the core of what it actually takes to develop a successful career in the music industry.

Books on the music business presently available—Shemel and Krasilovsky's *This Business of Music*, Denisoff's *Solid*

Gold, and Stokes's very well written *Star-making Machinery* are among the better ones—simply don't have enough of the right kind of information for people just starting out. They do not present basic survival strategies, nor do they offer sufficient explanation of the steps people should take (after they've learned how to survive) in order to become successful. This book does.

The subject of this book—how to begin a career in the music business properly and get ahead—does not require massive chapters devoted to understanding sophisticated concepts. Frankly, there aren't any sophisticated concepts in the music business. Nine-tenths of success is knowing the right people; one-tenth of success is having good products to sell. I'll spend my time advising readers how to plan their careers and develop invaluable connections rather than how to understand the intricacies of a fifty-two page recording agreement. Which subject is fundamentally more important, anyway? A recording contract is worthless if the record doesn't sell (this is a function of how good the artist's record company is, which we shall study). A graduate degree in marketing may look nice on the wall, or as an entry on a student's resume. However, in today's business it may almost be a hindrance for a person to study marketing in college, such is the propensity at some companies for fresh-scrubbed, prejudice-free trainees. This, too, we shall study.

The error (I might almost say guile) of music business educators until now has been to design training programs for aspiring music business professionals that are heavy on minute details but woefully short on delivering jobs, contracts, and profits. In particular, they fail to develop the sense of style (some might say pizzazz) that accompanies a getting-ahead success story. Learning how to survive and thrive is not a popular subject in academia. Talking too realistically about one's chances in the music business would undoubtedly force some developing institutions out of business. But survival training is of fundamental importance. To the best of my knowledge, this basic handbook on how to survive and become successful is a premier effort in reality-oriented education for the music business.

What does it mean to teach survival? It means getting down to basics. It means cutting through layer upon layer of nonessential information and reminding readers that luck, talent, hard work, and whom you know (not what you know) get most people farther along in their careers than having a genius IQ. There is a framework for getting ahead in the music business, however, that I wish to share with my readers. There is a right way and a wrong way to formulate business plans, to contact people in person or over the telephone, to enter into a deal, to pull out of a deal, and to go after private investors. And this is just scratching the surface of the content of this book.

I think you'll quickly see the difference in my approach. Every author, after all, has his own self-interest at heart. Music business lawyers write books about contracts. Journalists write stories about the biggest-name artists they can find, hoping in that way to sell more newspapers, books, or magazines. My self-interest is writing a book that will help every aspiring music business employee, from artist to mail clerk, learn not only how to survive but how to get ahead. It's not the most glamorous story in the world, but it's certainly important if you need answers.

One of the things I've learned from teaching more than 1,000 students is that the majority of aspiring music business professionals are basically nonreaders. I have decided, therefore, to organize my thoughts in a way that delivers the message quickly and effectively, but without heavy-handed treatment.

Each section of this book (they're all very short) carries an important tip as its title. The best way to use the book, after one or two thorough readings, is as a handy reference for advice prior to meeting a potential music business associate.

If just one section heading reminds you of an important approach to take—if a quick reading of related sections on shopping around for a record company, personal manager, or music publisher helps you see the contemplated relationship in a more realistic way—if this book helps you say the right thing instead of the wrong thing—then it will have done its job.

Throughout, I have written primarily in second and third person singular. Second person is "you"; third person singular is "he," "she," or "it." For the sake of brevity, I have chosen to use the word "he" when I might just as well use "she." I am well aware that close to 50 percent of my readers are female, and that practically all of the situations I have described are available today—rightly so—to women.

One other preliminary comment with reference to words should be made. The words "beginner," "new," "aspiring," and "newcomer" often recur in the following pages. It would be wrong, however, to conclude that *Getting Ahead in the Music Business* is intended only for raw beginners. Quite the contrary. It is intended not only to help literal beginners get started the right way but to help seasoned professionals (including artists, composers, managers, and agents) come to grips with why, after ten or twenty years, their careers may still not be in high gear. Please, do not interpret the word "beginner" in a negative or snobbish sense. If it defines your rudimentary understanding of the business and how to become successful (and it very well may), you'll just have to accept it, even if chronologically you haven't been a "beginner" (i.e., a spring chicken) for many years.

I shall assume that most of my readers are in some way familiar with the different elements and personalities in the music business; if not, you will learn a great deal as you go along. This book should help you perceive the music business for what it really is, not what it's reputed to be or what it's supposed to be. To the extent that you can assimilate this reality-oriented information into your own career plans, it should help improve your chances for getting ahead.

Are there still opportunities for becoming a superstar artist, composer, manager, agent, or promoter today? Yes, there are! But you do have to know some of the success secrets. So let's begin.

INTRODUCTION

The Ten Most Important Success Tips

After reading this book, you may realize as never before what a challenge it is to attempt a career in the music business today. Competition is fierce. You may have absolutely no connections at the beginning, and you probably don't have any money to invest. You will need all the encouragement and good advice you can get. When you need them the most, remember these ten most important tips on becoming successful:

1. Never give up. If *you* don't believe you can do it, you won't be able to convince anyone else, either. Pull off the road when you're really down. Do whatever it takes to start feeling superpositive once again. But you must keep going. You must believe in yourself totally. If you are talented, considerate of other people, and willing to pay your dues, you will ultimately succeed. If you don't have that kind of blind faith in yourself, you might as well get out of the business.

2. *Be yourself.*   You're not going to change, so you might as well accept who you are, how talented you are, and what your limitations are. The primary reason so many people fail is that they never stop to examine themselves and their motives. They never figure out what they're really all about. Without the inner strength gained from knowing yourself and assessing your true talent spectrum, your pursuit of a music business career will be farcical.

3. *Always ask questions.*   Every situation—especially those involving demo tapes, management services, or starting a company—is a learning opportunity for the beginner. If a person is disinterested, open your mouth and ask, "Why aren't you interested?" If you don't understand something, then say so. Getting answers to questions from music business professionals is the best way to learn the business and to garner free advice from those who have already made the mistakes you want to avoid.

4. *Work, work, work.*   Successful music business personalities are tireless human beings. Especially at the beginning level, you must constantly strive to expose yourself to the marketplace. People won't know how good you are unless you play for them, or sell them, or hustle them for money. It's up to you to get the word out, and the way to do it is to work your tail off. Quite a few people make it in this world on sheer energy.

5. *Be a team player.*   No one in this business makes it by himself (even Elvis Presley had Colonel Parker). When you're out seeking teammates, remember that it has to be a total team effort. Everyone has to pull his own weight for the team to score. Each member of the team has to have respect for the other members of the team. Without a true spirit of teamwork and camaraderie, there will be anarchy and your career will go no place.

6. *Know your place—Don't push too hard.* Learn to be patient at the beginning. You're not that important yet. Your value to a company is still unknown. If a company is interested in talking with you, that's wonderful. But don't push your luck. With one swat, you can be flicked outside the door again.

7. *Be a two-way thinker.* Learn to visualize a relationship from both sides, first your own, then the other person's. If you want an advance, consider how you would feel about giving it if the tables were turned. Try to be totally objective, and think for the other person, too. This two-way method of thinking is an invaluable survival technique.

8. *Let money be your last consideration.* Getting into the business is the only thing that matters at the start. Forget about money; it's bound to come if you're talented and if your career is handled well. Your energies should be focused on perfecting whatever creative skills you have; getting yourself known by the right people; and developing the best possible management team.

9. *Try not to create enemies.* One's personal reputation is a key asset in the music business. Learn to control your temper. Be careful what you say about other people. The person you sling verbal abuse at today might be the same person you want to approach next year. Keep your lines of communication open to as many potential music business associates as possible.

10. *Learn to deal from strength.* Save yourself the wear and tear of selling bad ideas or worthless tapes. Make sure your product is excellent. Merely good product isn't good enough—it has to be great. When you've got that type of product to sell, then you're ready to take on the music business.

PART 1

Getting Started

1

Find Out Who to Call

When you are just beginning your quest to become successful, you must have access to names, addresses, and telephone numbers of major music business companies and
their key employees. Scores of directories exist, but there are
three that I recommend as basic library editions:

Billboard International Buyer's Guide (published annually)—contains a complete listing of major U.S. and international record companies, music publishers, wholesalers
(including distributors, one-stops, rackjobbers, importers,
and exporters), music business service organizations, and
sheet music jobbers and suppliers. Send $35 to Billboard
Buyer's Guide, 2160 Patterson Street, Cincinnati, Ohio
45214.*

*Prices quoted are for directories published in 1978.

Billboard International Talent Directory (published annually)—contains a complete listing of major U.S. and international recording artists (including the artist's record company, booking agent, and personal manager); booking agents and contacts; personal managers; campus facilities, festivals, and state fairs; and a state-by-state listing of concert promoters, facilities, charter services, rental services (for limousines, musical instruments, portable stages, costumes, and sound and lights), unions, rehearsal studios, and ticket printing services. Send $25 to Billboard Talent Directory, 2160 Patterson Street, Cincinnati, Ohio 45214.

Billboard International Recording Equipment and Studio Directory (published annually)—contains a complete listing of major U.S. and international recording studios and rates, independent record producers, tape manufacturers, and schools offering recording courses. Send $15 to Billboard Recording Equipment Directory, 2160 Patterson Street, Cincinnati, Ohio 45214.

These three directories cover the major record companies, music publishers, independent record producers, recording studios, personal managers, booking agents, concert promoters, distributors, and pop music service organizations.

A complete listing of commercial jingles producers is contained in the *Back Stage TV Film/Tape and Syndication Directory* (published annually—send $6 to Back Stage Publications, 165 West 46 Street, New York, N.Y. 10036). There is also, for students of classical music, a complete U.S. and international listing of orchestras, opera companies, music festivals, classical music publishers, and artist managers in the *Musical America International Directory of the Performing Arts* (published annually—send $18 to Musical America, 130 East 59 Street, New York, N.Y. 10022).

It is a good idea to subscribe to at least one music industry trade magazine. The choices are *Billboard, Cashbox, Radio and Record,* and *Record World Magazine.* Each magazine annually publishes its own music industry directories and includes them in the price of a subscription (e.g., for $85 you would receive fifty-two issues of *Billboard* plus the *Billboard International Buyer's Guide,* the *Billboard International Talent Directory,* and the *Billboard International Recording Equipment and Studio Directory*).

Armed with the directories mentioned above and at least one trade magazine subscription, you will at least know who to contact when you're ready.

2

Have a Resume, Just in Case

Only very large companies with full-scale personnel departments are concerned about resumes in the music business. Smaller companies hire new employees on the basis of friendship, family ties, in-house personal recommendations, or the gut feelings of key executives. Practically all middle- and upper-level management people are hired on the basis of job experience, personal reputation, and how well connected the prospective employee is in the industry. Still, though you may never be asked to produce a resume, it's important that you have one just in case.

Resumes should be understated, brief, and impeccably typed. Typewriter type is fine—I myself turn off when I see a resume that's too ornate—but don't scrimp on the quality of the paper.

At the top of the resume, center your name, address, and telephone number. In the body of the resume list your edu-

10

cational background, work experience (including salaries), and personal information (e.g., age, marital status, children, hobbies).

Mailing unsolicited resumes is a complete waste of postage, paper, and time. People get jobs because they persist in hanging around in person, or because they have a friend on the inside. But for job interviews conducted at the request of an employer, it is advisable to have a resume ready for inspection.

3

Have Complete, Low-cost Demos Made

Demonstration tapes (not discs) are the calling cards of the music business. Artists, songwriters, producers, and managers must have them. Here is the way to prepare them:

1. Songwriter demos should be very clean and simple. A vocalist with guitar accompaniment is preferred. No matter what anyone tells you, there is absolutely no need to spend hundreds of dollars on songwriter demos if you have a half-way decent tape recorder at home and a quiet room in which to record.

2. Artist and producer demos can also be taped at home if the artists perform "live"—i.e., all together at the same time. However, if an artist wishes to demonstrate a multi-faceted talent spectrum, such as playing every instrument and singing all the vocals on the recording, the demo should be produced at a professional recording studio.

3. If a professional recording studio is necessary, consult the *Billboard International Recording Equipment and Studio Directory* or local music services publications for names, addresses, and telephone numbers of at least three potential studios. Shop around for the best price, and remember the cardinal rule for saving money as a recording artist or producer: NEVER REHEARSE IN THE STUDIO— ALWAYS BE PREPARED.

4. Put no more than four songs on a demo.

5. Don't go overboard on demo copies. A half-dozen duplicates will do for a start. Make sure you get them back from the record companies, publishers, and managers you send them to. (Note: This shouldn't be too much of a problem—if you follow my advice, you'll send out demo tapes only after establishing contact with a company employee [usually a secretary] who will return your tape on request.)

6. Put leader tape between the songs on the recording so that listeners can find the start of a new selection quickly.

7. Put identification labels on the front and back of the tape box, and on the tape reel itself. The label should include the name of the artist, a listing of selections, and the name, address, and telephone number of the songwriter or artist's representative.

8. If there are words to the music, type out a lyric sheet, have it reduced at your local copy center, and paste the lyrics to the inside and outside of the reel-to-reel tape box.

9. Include a copyright notice (© followed by your name and the year in which you completed the song) at the top of each set of lyrics. You do not, however, have to register copyrights of the songs with the U.S. Copyright Office at this time.

10. Include a phonorecord notice (℗ followed by your name and the year in which you completed the demo) on the front of the tape box and the label of the tape reel. Again, I do not recommend registering copyrights (in this case, for a phonorecord) until there is a need to. When a

record company releases your recording or a publisher signs you to a publishing contract is the time to be concerned about filing copyright registrations.

11. Lead sheets are not necessary. Neither are reviews or photographs of the artist or composer. What counts is how good the lyrics and melody are, if you're a songwriter; how good the act performs, if you're a group or solo artist; or how professional the tape sounds, if you're a producer. In the music business, music is still very much the bottom line.

4

Get a Music Business Lawyer

The music business is dense with contracts. Initially, you will need a lawyer to decipher these agreements for you. Later you will need a lawyer to act as a contract negotiator, manager of your finances, and as a general business adviser. The best time to line up a good music business lawyer is before you actually need one.

New York City and Los Angeles are currently swimming in music business attorneys. It's not uncommon for clients living in Nashville, Tulsa, or, for that matter, New York City to have a Los Angeles-based legal adviser, or for Los Angeles-based clients to be represented by a New York City firm. The difficulty, if you don't have a relative in the legal profession, is getting through to lawyers as a completely unattached outsider. Clues on which firms to contact are provided every week in trade publication stories. Other likely places for contact information on firms (not individual lawyers) are the American Society of Composers, Authors, and Publishers (ASCAP); Broadcast Music Inc. (BMI); SESAC (this is the official name of the organization and is pronounced "SEA-sack"); the American Guild of Authors and Composers (AGAC); and the Practicing Law Institute (ask which firms attend PLI courses dealing with copyright and the entertainment business).

It's a relatively simple step to go from the name and telephone number of a firm to the name of an individual attorney at the firm who specializes in the music business. Be nice to the receptionist, and you'll be connected to that lawyer's secretary.

When you've reached that point, you must have something specific to talk about. I would suggest you say the following: first, you are calling the lawyer at the recommendation of a reputable music business association or individual. Second, you want to find out if Mr. or Ms. Attorney (the secretary's boss) would be interested in representing you if a potential deal comes through in the near future. Tell the secretary what rounds you've made, which companies are listening (supposedly) to your tapes, and when you're supposed to get an answer, one way or the other, on whether the company or companies are going to offer you a contract.

If your act is together and you're mentioning established companies, you should be able to impress the secretary sufficiently to get through to the boss. If not, hang up, dial the firm again, and ask the receptionist to put you through to another music business lawyer (with a different secretary). Go through one law firm completely before tackling another firm.

Most of the lawyers I know in the music business actually bend over backwards to help newcomers. Many of them hold off charging new clients until the client can afford to pay partial attorney fees. Be wary, however, of lawyers who offer to work for a percentage in lieu of hourly charges—if you make it to the top, you're going to regret having to pay your lawyer a percentage of net income rather than a monthly retainer.

What turns lawyers and their secretaries off to potential new clients is an amateur performance on the telephone. You must say something specific and positive. Don't say, "Is it true that the copyright law was recently changed?" or something else that will be considered insipid.

Of course, the most unforgivable mistake in dealing with lawyers is to ask for free legal advice over the telephone on an initial inquiry. If you play your cards right, there really shouldn't be any problem getting at least one music business lawyer to accept you as a client. But if it's not working, don't blame the lawyer—blame yourself. You're not fully prepared yet, so keep trying (but don't bother the lawyer again until you're ready).

5

Get the Right
Kind of Education

It's easy to say, "Learn how to do it first." But it's not so easy
to get the right kind of education for entering the music
business.

Many of the most important music business executives,
including company owners, never went to college. Quite a
number of marketing, finance, and merchandising heads of
record companies do not have college degrees in their areas
of business expertise. Many record and publishing companies prefer hiring new employees without preconceived
ideas of how a record or publishing company should be run.
What this means is that the music business does not subscribe to the fundamental importance (for most other professions) of getting a college education first.

For me, the ideal music business education is a job—any
job to start—within the industry. Nothing teaches better
than actual work experience. Nothing advances music bus-

iness employees faster than being in the environment and being perceived as a talented newcomer, eager to learn.

Harvard M.B.A.'s may be yearning for the marketing job swept away by a person who literally started at the company as a floor sweeper. The place to be is inside the industry. The place not to be for any considerable length of time—unless you're studying law, accounting, business, or journalism—is an expensive undergraduate or graduate school. This, of course, is my personal view; I don't expect everyone to share it equally.

In defense of higher education, I will say that most record and publishing company executives that I know are impressed with job candidates who went to college for at least a few years. It's too early to tell what impact professional music business schools, such as the Zadoc Institute for Practical Learning (which I founded) or the University of Miami's music merchandising school, will have. They may one day be accepted as recruitment centers for new music business employees if graduates of these schools show an exceptional aptitude for working in the industry.

If nothing else, I think music business professional schools provide a valuable contact service for students interested in breaking into the business. A number of my more aggressive students are now working in the music business because they persuaded an executive guest speaker to hire them.

Songwriting, performing, promotion, and sales are highly personalized skills better learned—if they can be at all—outside the college environment. Books, newspaper articles, and certainly trade publications can fill in a lot of informational gaps about the music business at a fraction of the cost of graduate college education.

In short, the best environment for learning the music business is the music business itself. It's out there, and it always has room for truly gifted newcomers. Getting in and staying in will be the next subject in our discussion of what it takes to succeed in the music business.

PART 2

Survival Strategies

6

Develop Survival Skills

Learning how to survive is the foundation of a successful career. It is a very basic subject. It is also a *different* subject (in the sense that arithmetic is different from calculus) than learning how to become successful. Let us be different from the great majority of people who think they know what they're doing, but are doing it backward. Let's study survival first; then we'll learn how to apply survival skills toward the development of a successful career.

People coming into the music business totally on their own are just that—alone. They will either be treated with persistent rudeness or their very existence will go unnoticed. Most beginners don't even make it into the legitimate music business of major record companies and artist representatives on their first try. Instead, they obtain a tenuous foothold in that subuniverse which for lack of a better term I'll call the "music business jungle." (Note: As a former Juilliard student, concert pianist, conductor, and empresario, I can assure you that the jungle does exist.)

Your goal as a jungle inhabitant is to be a survivor. Here are some preliminary tips on getting out of the jungle quickly:

1. Forget your illusions.   Forget what you've read about the music business in the trades. Forget the glamour, forget the money, forget the sex, forget everything. You want the world, but first you have to start paying your dues.

2. Accept the jungle order for what it is.   Don't fight it— embrace it. Learn from it. Let it toughen you; let it mold your future plans. You will never totally escape the jungle, but in time you may learn how to spend most of your life outside of it.

3. Guard your ideas.   Everybody steals in the jungle if he can. Save your ideas for privileged members of your team. Be wary of strangers. Make staying alive in the music business the most important thing in your daily routine.

4. Find work in your profession.   Aspiring artists don't need record companies yet—they need a smart booking agent. Aspiring songwriters don't need publishers yet—they need secretarial jobs by day and songwriter showcase opportunities by night. Aspiring personal managers and agents need fresh, new acts to work with; each may learn from the other's mistakes. Aspiring concert promoters need access to small clubs and a hook for baiting talent, such as a weeknight talent showcase. It's small potatoes, it's crazy, but it's real life.

5. Forget about contracts.   It's all word of mouth when you start up (at least it should be—if a jungle predator approaches you with a binding written contract, walk away). Learn to read the signs on people's faces. Ask questions. Think very, very carefully about what's being offered. But once you've made up your mind, do it. If you back off, you'll get the reputation for being a rat.

6. Immerse yourself in the business.   Make it an eighteen-hour-a-day happening. The more you're in it, the faster you'll learn the ropes. If you can't take the pace, get out.

These are just preliminary words of advice on the underground world I call the music business jungle. It's a subindustry that deserves more space in the music business trades. It's the place where practically every music business superstar got started. But the music business jungle doesn't read well. Frankly, it's dirty.

The music business jungle doesn't provide minimum union scale wages (if it pays at all). It's been known to siphon millions of dollars out of thousands of victimized youngsters for useless demonstration tapes, trumped-up personal or business management services, and unnecessary showcase concerts. It's the place before all other places in the business where the buyer must beware.

But the music business jungle is the most valuable testing laboratory for music business people. It's the place to begin sorting out your ambitions, talent, and realistic goals. You can get out of the jungle, provided you're lucky and smart.

Expect to make mistakes when you're starting out. Everybody's made them. Above all, learn to be patient. Don't expect overnight miracles to occur—that's what seems to be happening to people you read about in the trades, but it only appears to be that way. Practically everyone who makes any news splash has been paying dues for years.

It's the jungle survivors who get ahead. And survival starts with the understanding that the jungle is a lot bigger than you. You're not going to change it. Your only hope is to learn how to deal with it in the manner that is expected, and thereby to survive.

7

Choose Your Teammates Carefully

One of the music business survival skills most often overlooked has nothing to do with music. It's the ability to select
a cohesive fighting unit. It's the talent, native to relatively
few individuals, for choosing long-term, artistically creative, responsible allies. Luck has a lot to do with the formation of a superteam, but there are also guidelines that apply
to the formation of any music business assembly numbering
more than one individual.

Each group should have one recognized team leader. The
leader must be superaggressive, business oriented, and willing to take care of himself and the group in clinches.

The members of the team must have respect for each
other. Most teams would also be well advised to keep their
interpersonal relationships on a professional basis. The jun-

gle is not the place to disintegrate as the result of a broken heart.

In selecting a key business comrade—either a manager, agent, concert promoter, or any combination of the three—the choice should be based on which person can get the group the most EXPOSURE. Relatively few potential business teammates understand that readiness, which in turn is a function of how comfortable the group feels in front of an audience, is more important a virtue than cutting a twenty-four-track demo whose songs aren't salable.

At least one of the members of the group—preferably the team leader—should have access to some degree of financing. Money is essential, sooner or later, in the music business. However, I think it is a mistake for new groups to invest a lot of money in their own careers (i.e., it would be better to let someone else take the financial risk, if a backer can be found).

The jungle period is not the time to be overly concerned about the group's music. I have spent a lot of time in New York's Greenwich Village and on The Strip in Hollywood, and my suspicions are continuously reaffirmed that, especially for newly established teams, being very aggressive is the most important factor in getting initial exposure.

Incidentally, the second most important factor isn't how well the group plays, either. It's whether the group carries its own instruments, thereby freeing the club owner from the onus of having to rent equipment.

Acts that are, at best, mediocre can forge ahead on the basis of persistent, hard-nosed selling. The team leader must become known to the talent coordinators of amateur-night clubs. It is also the leader's job to ferret out songwriter showcase opportunities if the group composes original melodies.

Not until the fringes of the jungle are reached does pure musical talent begin to play a decisive role in the selection of players who will rise above the other contenders. Until then, the accent in music business development is on BUSINESS. If you have a group, if you're self-contained, if you have an aggressive leader and you sound halfway decent, your tuition will have been paid. Then it's up to you to learn from your audience how to make appealing music.

8

Establish Who Owns What

I hope that one of the most painful lessons associated with entering the music business will be avoided after reading this section.

As soon as you begin creating music or anything else in a group setting—even if it's just you and a casual acquaintance you don't see again for ten years—there arises the legitimate question of ownership. The song you just composed, for example—did each member of the group contribute to it equally? Did one member of the group write it exclusively? Did one member of the group contribute the music and two members of the group write the lyrics, or was it the other way around?

What about the arrangement of the song—who wrote that? And what about all the other songs that were created from the collective group experience?

What about the name of the group? Did the group invent

the name, or did a member of the group invent the name? Who owns that name? What would happen if a member of the group decided to split, but not without taking the group's name with him and using it for his new act? Would this be agreeable to the members of the original group or not?

What about the logo of the group, or any artwork that identifies that particular group? What about costumes, makeup, or special vocal effects created during the getting-it-together stage—who owns them?

Who owns the group's instruments? Is it, in fact, a group, or is it an assembly of individuals calling themselves a group, but without legal justification for doing so? These are the types of questions to be dealt with before too much time has passed in the formation of a music business team. It is preferable that there be a written understanding (it doesn't have to be a contract; a notarized statement or letter of intent will do) among the members of the group concerning these and other matters.

It may not be necessary at this time to incorporate the group or even to consult with a music business lawyer. But having who owns what in writing is in everyone's long-term mutual best interest.

Too often someone gets ripped off down the line over a hit song whose origins were never clearly established. There is also, at this time, the matter of outside participation to ponder, since quite a number of groups cannot get going strictly by themselves.

If a friend of the group is acting as a manager, financier, promoter, or anything else relating to the development and continuation of that group, an identification label should be attached to that friend's role (e.g., "John Doe gave our group the idea for this song"), along with a valuation for the friend's services (e.g., 20 percent of concert income; a finder's fee for placing the group with an established manager, producer, or record company; complete reimbursement for the friend's out-of-pocket expenses relating to the group). Sliding scales are often used in these cases, with the friend's financial interest rising as his investment in time and money on behalf of the group goes up.

Let me reiterate that the jelling of a group should be done quietly and with circumspection. But behind the creative process, there must always be a subliminal awareness that your group might get lucky and strike it rich. If that happens, everyone in the group should know the score.

9

Don't Register Copyrights until There's a Need To

For a number of reasons, this advice probably sounds like heresy to most readers. First, there is my earlier statement that everybody steals in the jungle. Second, there is the knowledge culled from reading the trades that copyright infringement is, indeed, a major international problem. Third, on a more personal, subjective level, there is the secret hope, harbored by virtually every songwriter, that the song they just composed is destined to become a hit. This fantasy reasoning, in particular, doesn't jibe with reality. The music business jungle may be a lot of things, but one thing it definitely isn't is a dreamworld.

Of the various parasites who prey on innocent young songwriters, the most odious would seem to be the professional song shark. The song shark is not actually concerned with how good the song is, but with whether a victim's $200 or $300 check will bounce. The song shark's trade, which is to prepare lead sheets, manufacture singles, and distribute these to obscure secondary and tertiary radio stations that promptly throw them away, does not interface with the legitimate music publishing world in any way. No business person—including the song shark—gives a damn about a lousy song. I do not say this to condone the actions of what for many years has been a successful con game. Let's just say I'm tired of hearing so many copyright-related professional organizations preach song-shark paranoia as a valid reason for membership.

If you write good songs, you will discover that participants in the legitimate music business don't want to steal from you—they want to get involved with you. They want to marry you and your songs. They want an honest piece of the action, now and forever. Other songwriters and performers may lift ideas occasionally from your work (one hopes from your better work), but so what? Every author "steals" from every other author, though it's hardly the same thing as copying, note for note and word for word, the melody and lyrics of another person. Among other things, it takes a real talent to do that without a tape recorder. And with or without the tape recorder, it is also illegal to make exact duplicates.

Generally speaking, it is a waste of money to register copyrights of songs before you have a publisher. As for the copyright infringement actions covered in your weekly trade paper, they are not applicable to the world of the music business jungle. The participants in these mock clashes (rarely do they go to court) are fighting over alleged mechanical royalties due, increased performing rights fees, and the failure to obtain adequate writer identification permissions for songwriter folios. When and if you ever make it to the big leagues, these copyright infringement matters may legitimately concern you, but not before.

The five points that follow constitute a bare-bones advisory on copyrights:

1. Always use a copyright notice.   Be sure that a proper copyright notice (© followed by your name and the year in which you completed the song) appears at the bottom of the first page of printed music.

2. Don't sell copies of the work yourself   (copies include lead sheets, sheet music, phonograph records, and tapes). First, it is a colossal waste of money to manufacture copies if you're a raw beginner. Second, when you sell a work you are "publishing" the work, and you will need to register the copyright with the U.S. Copyright Office for adequate protection from infringement.

3. Don't get involved with song sharks.   Their trademark is the little newspaper ad that reads, "Send Us Your Songs."

4. Prepare for the future.   Learn the names of the major U.S. publishing firms, using the *Billboard International Buyer's Guide* as a reference.

5. Know the score.   Most copyrights are worthless because the songs attached to them are not publishable. Until you are approached by a major publisher or a rising young publisher, your energies should not be focused on registering copyrights. The exclusive focus of your time and money should be on perfecting your craft and exposing it in the marketplace.

10

The Secret to Success Is Planning

I think this is the most important lesson to be learned from reading this book. Learn how to plan your music career. Discover how much time it's going to take to do something; how much money it's going to cost; how many steps are involved in accomplishing the objective; what the risks are; and what the positive benefits would be for you and your colleagues if the plan were to succeed. All this should be done BEFORE you go out and try your luck.

Musicians, as a rule, are incredibly inept at planning anything. This is not surprising, as the pursuit of musical knowledge has until recently been entrusted to arts-oriented instrumental and theory teachers whose business acumen (I will be kind) is underdeveloped. Planning, at least, is a learnable skill for most people. It's easy to discuss how business planning should be done; the hard part is to get into the habit of doing it. But planning can make a world of difference. It gives direction and focus to your career. It forces you to be objective. The more you know about planning, the less likely it is that you'll perish in the music business jungle.

Although planning your career will not guarantee success, one can safely argue that planning never hurt anyone. It's certainly done CBS, Warner Communications, and RCA a world of good, just to mention three of the major entertainment conglomerates in the world.

The major criticism against planning is that, many times, plans are left by the wayside. If so, there should be a backup or contingency plan to insert in place of the original plan.

In the music business there is a large clique that doesn't subscribe to planning, but rather to gut feeling, "vibes," or personal astrology charts. Still, planning is an essential, and probably the most important, survival tool. It is the most painless way for getting to know yourself and your limitations.

Particularly if you're a gambler by nature, you owe it to yourself to read sections 11 through 17 of this book very carefully.

11

Plan Your Time Properly

Start by planning your time. You must constantly ask yourself at every important juncture in your career, "Is this the best possible utilization of my time?" "Should I spend 100 percent of my time trying to be successful at one particular thing, or should I split myself up, perhaps 50–50 or 60–40, between what I want to do and what I need to do in order to make a living?"

Once again, I am a strong believer in the fallacy of going to college for a music business education, unless you want to be an accountant, lawyer, or marketing maven. I am appalled that so many young people are enrolling in four-year music business degree programs in such out-of-the-way cities—for the music business, that is—as Syracuse (Syracuse University), Atlanta (Georgia State University), and Miami (University of Miami).

Four years is an incredibly long time to spend learning

this rather elementary business where, in any case, who you know is much more important than what you know. I'd much rather see young people, if they've decided that they want a music business career, not only immerse themselves in the jungle habitat (assuming this is the best they can do at the beginning), but also persistently try to get a job in the neighboring, legitimate music business.

All low-level music business jobs must be viewed primarily as alternative college education. If the "course" (i.e., the job) you have isn't getting you ahead, either in terms of pure knowledge or advancement within the company, then you should politely cut out (always do it gracefully, however; a good referral may come in handy later on).

Ideally, you'll want to begin working for a major music business entity like a booking agency, music publishing company, or record company where opportunities exist to make contact with VIP's throughout the industry. If you're not working for a major company, you may be wasting your time. If you're not doing what you want to do but you're nevertheless working for a major company and meeting the right people, my advice is to stay with it a while longer. What you want to do may not always be what would be best for you to do. Maximize your odds for success by becoming known to top people within the industry and letting them see what you're capable of doing.

How you work will tell a lot about your ultimate chances for becoming successful. No matter what the job—and I can't begin to tell you how many presidents of major companies started out in the mail room—you should exude a spirit of positive goodwill. Don't walk around with a chip on your shoulder. Somebody did you a favor by letting you work inside that particular company, and you should be grateful.

All you have to do to prove this to yourself is to ask various department heads inside the company what they did before they got their present jobs. Then you'll see how most people move up the ladder in the music business. It starts at the ground floor with a low-paying, point-of-entry job. Then, if the individual is intelligent, eager to work, and able to handle the daily crises of being in the music business, advancement can come rapidly and with wondrous financial rewards.

If you're really good, within four years you will have left the jungle habitat permanently, and you will either be heading up your own department within the company or be making real progress as a professional songwriter or recording artist. By then, you may be literally "in the money."

12

Give Yourself a Purpose, and Keep It Narrow

Take a tip from the professional fund-raising community. Give yourself a purpose for existing. Become, in your own mind at least, a corporate entity. And keep your purpose narrow to begin: you're only one person, and there are only so many hours in a day for work.

Compressing one's career objectives into a statement of twenty-five words or less may seem to the uninitiated to be a wasteful exercise. Well, try it. Put your career aspirations in writing. Then ask yourself, "Does what I wrote make sense? Is it possible for me to achieve my goals? If so, how?"

If your purpose truly is to do everything, you will almost certainly succeed at doing nothing. Before you can run, you must walk. Before you can do *more* than one thing in the music business, you must be regarded as being very proficient at that one thing. Only step by step is it possible to make your way in the music business jungle.

What it is you want to do the most should become your purpose for being in the music business. Then, it is extremely important that you STAY WITH IT and not get sidetracked.

Be highly self-critical and in a commonsense mood when formulating your purpose for being in the music business. Make sure what you want to do is something for which you have an aptitude, and not just something that you'd like to do. Remember that you're only one person: you can't be in two places at the same time, and you can't excel at one thing if you're working hard at three things and not getting adequate rest.

It is anathema to mix business purposes, such as management, promotion, and record production, with so-called creative purposes, such as songwriting and performance. Each separate element of the music business will require an inordinate amount of time and money to get off the ground. Writers and artists may be tempted to go the route of the singer-songwriter, which is possible provided the individual is highly gifted in both areas. Otherwise, I would strongly recommend concentrating on either writing or performance—whichever the person likes doing more—at the outset of your career.

13

Set Attainable Goals for Yourself, Then Work Hard to Reach Them

Second only to establishing a purpose in business planning importance is a listing of attainable goals. An individual songwriter's achievement goal, for example, might be, "To have at least one of my songs signed by a major U.S. publishing firm within one year, with an accompanying advance." An individual manager's achievement goal might be, "To have my act signed to a major U.S. record company for a minimum advance of $25,000; also, to have my act signed to a major U.S. booking agency." An individual artist's achievement goal might be, "To make $20,000 after taxes within two years; to make $25,000 after taxes within three years; to make $30,000 after taxes within four years."

Goals keyed to financial achievement levels are, in my opinion, highly desirable. The minimum one should expect from a long-term professional career in the music business is a decent living. Give yourself that income, insofar as plan-

42

ning is concerned. Don't expect to make $500,000 for your first three years in the business, but don't feel benign about making zero in all that time (zero from what you want to do in the music business, that is), either.

If I were to embark on a career in the music business today, I wouldn't be overly concerned with who I was signed to, or who my producer was, or how many pictures I had in my scrapbook. My overriding concern would be to make at least $20,000 a year gross income from combined music business sources. I've learned that you can't use the name of a record company to buy a new car, or a picture of yourself with a superstar to entice money out of bank loan officers. Money matters most, if you're interested in living nicely. I suggest, therefore, that you begin to think primarily in terms of achieving financial goals rather than achieving goals based entirely on status.

Once the goal is set, it's up to you to go out and attain it (and even surpass it). Aspiring music business professionals should establish annual benchmarks for themselves, and pay particular attention to how close they've actually come to attaining their goal. If it's not working—if you're not making a decent living—the efficacy of the business plan must be reexamined carefully.

14

Establish Who Should Be Members of Your Business Team, and How Much They Cost

The idea here is to pinpoint your minimum support-personnel needs and compute how much money that support will cost IN ADVANCE of its costing you anything.

A beginning artist's minimum support team consists of backup players and a booking agent. Backup players are usually gotten for free by offering them partnerships in the act. An agency, however, will assess the act either 10 or 15 percent of the monies it receives for getting the act a concert, or gig.

A beginning songwriter's minimum support team consists of at least one act willing to perform the songwriter's compositions. Such gestures are usually made on the basis of friendship, although some acts will ask for a percentage of earnings on songs they help become hits through the exposure they provide.

A beginning personal manager's minimum support team

consists of at least one act for which he is supplying exclusive representation. The manager may have to spend a lot of money getting the act ready for professional recordings and live appearances.

A beginning agent's minimum support team consists of at least one act—preferably a name act that can command instant bookings—under his exclusive representation. One of the most attractive things about the agency business is that it doesn't cost a lot of money to get into. (Fore example, Frank Barsalona started the most successful contemporary music agency in the world, Premier Talent, with an investment of $50.)

A beginning concert promoter's minimum support team consists of a club owner willing to have concerts featured at his club under the promoter's auspices. Initially, concert promotion doesn't require a large capital investment, but as soon as talent negotiations begin with established booking agents, the promoter must be able to invest thousands of dollars.

A beginning publisher's support team consists of at least one songwriter willing to pass copyrights over to the publisher. A publisher's initial out-of-pocket expenses are for demos, letterheads, and a telephone.

On the other hand, a beginning record company owner's support team consists of at least one recording artist, a national distribution network, a promotions director, and a secretary. Butterfly Records, one of the few successful new labels to emerge in 1978, began with a capitalization of $500,000. Without that kind of investment backing, you should forget about starting a record company in today's business.

In each of these categories I have placed stress on the word "beginning." There is an enormous difference in the level of support personnel required by an established music business entity in comparison to what the beginner needs, bare-bones, to launch a career within the music business jungle. For beginners, however, it is advisable to travel lightly. Above all, don't bother reputable managers, agents, publishers, and record companies until you really have something to sell.

Not until you have established a foothold within the business (e.g., a regular club engagement; management representation of several noteworthy acts; or exclusive control of an important club, or venue) should you be concerned about supplementing the members of your creative or management team. Until then, you want to save as much money and control as much of your business as you possibly can.

15

Itemize the Facilities You Need; Then Find Something Cheaper

Four walls and a ceiling. No matter where it is—in Malibu or the Lower East Side, in a rehearsal room or a twenty-four-track professional recording studio—it's going to cost money. Unless, that is, you learn to think like an alley cat.

One of the most effective ways to reduce facility costs is by bartering. You may be able to rehearse for free in a community center, high school, or religious institution in exchange for a series of free concerts. Your group may be able to cut a demo for free in exchange for teaching the studio owner how to read music. Or you may be able to get a talent showcase fee waived by offering to put the promoter of the showcase in contact with a VIP music business executive.

Investigate not only rehearsal studios, but churches, schools, barns, hotel suites, and union halls. Find out whether there is an affinity among you, your music, and the manager of that facility. Then open your mouth and say, "I wonder if we might be able to work something out."

In my own career as a classical music director and conductor, I was able to rehearse for two years at the Riverside Church (an absolutely magnificent facility) in exchange for doing a series of children's concerts. Later, the orchestra I directed switched to rehearsing at the WQXR auditorium in the *New York Times* building. This also was in exchange for a series of live radio broadcasts on Robert Sherman's morning show.

When the orchestra performed at an elementary school, it naturally needed to rehearse several times in the school auditorium in order to "get the feel" of the hall. I had to make these facility arrangements because the Juilliard School, where I studied, wouldn't allow us to rehearse on its premises (technically we were a renegade, cooperative ensemble). But there were two positive results: I learned never to be afraid to ask for something, and I was able to tie the outside rehearsals and performances into fund-raising grants that kept the orchestra going for five years.

Saving money on facility rentals is one of the few remaining areas where beginners can cut budgetary corners. If you're paying for a facility, that's unfortunate. With a little bit of investigation and nerve, you might be able to get the facility for free.

16

Budget Your Income and Expenses; Then Compute the Bottom Line

Every business plan must ultimately be reduced to a dollars-and-cents computation of how much money the plan will generate. If the first three steps I've recommended in business planning are taken – if you've narrowed your purpose, projected attainable goals, and defined who the members of your business team will be – this exercise in budgeting and projecting financial earnings will be incredibly valuable. Otherwise, your figures will probably come out looking as deceptively rosy as your grandiose plans for changing the world, or at least becoming the next Elvis Presley. As always, I prefer dealing in facts rather than fiction.

There are three basic sources of income for newcomers to the music business. First is parental income, or its equivalent; second is music business income; third is full or part-time job income, assuming that music business income alone can't pay the rent. This income should be considered adjusted income if your employer has already taken out FICA, federal, state, and local taxes, or unadjusted gross income if no taxes are withheld from wages.

Against income, your expenses will include such mundane things as rent, telephone, utilities, clothing, food, medical expenses, insurance (if you have any), transportation, professional services (for legal fees and accountants), and educational services, for school tuition and books. Under music business expenses you should list the following: instrument purchases, instrument repair (includes broken strings), cartage, rehearsal facilities, demos, costumes, concert rentals, and finally management services (these percentage-of-earnings computations are based on what your agent or manager, if you have either, is entitled to receive as compensation for services performed).

If taxes have not been taken out of your wages (i.e., you have unadjusted gross income), you should take 25 percent of your total income and enter it as a tax expense. The difference between total income and total expenses, of course, is net income. The accompanying example shows how the financial statement will look in columnar form.

Let me reiterate that the jungle environment is not the place for factoring in record and publishing income. Records and publishing probably won't happen until your act is tight, terrific, and superprofessional. Until then, your budget should be keyed to what you can realistically expect to do with your career during the early years.

Projecting income and expense figures over a longer period of time (three to five years) is a salutary idea. Your realistic budget for the first year may be frightening. You might even be persuaded to get out of the music business after observing the probable bleakness of your first-year prospects.

But if you really want a career in the music business you have to give yourself that first year, and maybe the second, and maybe even a third. I think it would be unfair, though for artists, songwriters, and personal managers not to pro-

STATEMENT OF INCOME AND EXPENSE:
[YOUR NAME]

INCOME

Parental income (or its equivalent) . . . .
Music business income:
        Studio work . . . .
        Concerts . . . .
        Songwriting . . . .
        Arrangements . . . .
        Teaching. . . . .
        Other . . . .
Part-time or full-time job income . . . . _____

TOTAL ADJUSTED INCOME (FICA, federal, state, and local taxes withheld by employer) . . . . _____

EXPENSES

Rent . . . .
Telephone. . . . .
Utilities. . . . .
Clothing . . . .
Food . . . .
Medical. . . . .
Insurance . . . .
Transportation . . . .
Professional services . . . .
Educational services . . . .
Music business expenses:
        Instrument purchases . . . .
        Instrument repair . . . .
        Cartage. . . . .
        Rehearsal facilities . . . .
        Demos. . . . .
        Costumes . . . .
        Concert rentals . . . .
        Management services . . . .
        Other . . . .
Taxes (for people with unadjusted gross income) . . . . _____

TOTAL EXPENSES . . . . _____

_____

NET PROFIT (OR LOSS) . . . . _____

ject making more money in time (including royalties from phonograph records and publishers). Record studio owners, booking agents, and concert promoters should likewise project eventual upturns in their unadjusted gross income. Just don't expect the world when you're starting out alone.

17

Keep a List of Likely Investors (But Don't Call Them until You're Ready)

Potential record store owners, recording studio owners, independent record producers, concert promoters, personal managers, publishers, distributors, and artists may each one day require large capital expenditures in order to reach the next level in their careers. Fund-raising strategies will be covered shortly, but it would be inappropriate to leave the business planning section without mentioning how important it is always to plan for the next step forward.

From a fund-raising standpoint, the most important thing you will gain from starting your career in the jungle is EXPERIENCE. Survivors of these lean years can go to people and say, "I know what I'm talking about—I've lived the experience." If your record is impressive—if you can show an investor that not only did you survive but that you thrived within the jungle—your fund-raising proposal will be taken seriously. In ways such as this, the jungle experience is more helpful to its graduating class than a Bachelor of Arts degree (but no working experience) from Harvard, Yale, or any other Ivy League school.

Hold off on contacting potential investors until your business plan for a contemplated venture looks as solid as Gibralter. In the meantime, keep adding to your list of potential investors. Make friends and influence people as you go along. Try not to make enemies. But when you're actually talking to people about a $50,000 or $100,000 loan, you may feel differently about those incredibly difficult years in the music business jungle.

18

Convert Your Skills into High-paying Part-time Jobs

Playing music is, among other things, a practical skill. So is typing, shorthand, carpentry, painting, furniture repairing, antiquing, and being able to fix automobiles. Any of these jobs can pay more money than being a busboy or waiter, which is what so many aspiring music business individuals seem to do in order to make a living. Some of these skills, in fact, can be converted into part-time jobs that pay $15, $30, or even $50 an hour. If it's not too late you should get off your rear, learn one of these skills from scratch or perfect an existing skill, and discover how you, too, can maximize income while saving precious time.

Here is an example of what I mean by a convertible skill. There is a man who teaches courses in the music business at a leading southern university. Early in life, this man tried to start his own music publishing company, but he was not successful. In fact, he went into debt. Now this man had a hobby: he loved fixing old cars. He found that if he used authentic parts and fixed the cars up nicely, he could sell them to antique-car collectors for a fabulous profit. Today this man is a millionaire. He turned another hobby, building houses, into an even bigger part-time business. Yet he never turned his back completely on the music business. He is a tenured music business professor who converted practical skills into a magnificent annual income. To my way of thinking, this man demonstrates a bona fide success story.

You may not know how to build a house or fix a car. But you may still remember some shorthand from the eleventh grade. You may be interested in learning how to weave, how to bind books, or how to refinish old furniture. In short, you may either have the desire to learn or already possess some latent skill that can be converted into a high-paying part-time job—provided, however, you really try.

The difference in life style can be incredible. Instead of working forty hours a week, you can work ten hours. Instead of devoting ten hours a week to music, you can devote forty hours or more a week to music. You'll feel better, you'll have the potential for making a lot more money, and you'll meet a lot of interesting people along the way. The choice is yours: do you want to be a waiter, or would you rather move forward with your career as fast as you can?

19

Keep a Complete Record of Your Group's Expenses

It's the little expenses like cab fare, copies, postage stamps, photographs, and stationery that eventually hurt so many aspiring music business professionals in the pocketbook. Not only should a complete record of out-of-pocket expenses be kept; there should be a written understanding, signed by each member of the group, on who is ultimately responsible for paying the bills—the group, one or two members of the group, the manager, or some other possible combination.

If I were the person in charge of organizing a new group, I'd put together a correspondence file (incoming and outgoing mail) and a cash disbursements file. I'd get receipts for whatever purchases I make on behalf of the group, and I'd expect each member of the group periodically to pay back his or her fair share of the group's outstanding debt to me. (I might also argue that by acting as the group's bookkeeper I should either get paid $5 an hour, or have my personal debt to the group reduced by the number of hours I work. Of course, the other members of the group would have to pay a little bit more to make up the difference.)

I would also prepare a simple financial record and each month fill in how much money the group spent in the areas shown in the accompanying example.

An alternative approach is for each member of the group to contribute $10 or $15 a month toward a group checking account. Actually, this is a good way to train artists and composers to be sensible with money, but, as might be expected, most artists and composers are somewhat resistant not only to getting involved with finances, but also to parting with their hard-earned money.

This is hardly the time to be concerned about sheltering income (if there is any). What you want to establish is what it actually costs for the group to stay together during its formative stages. Then, if a record company one day expresses interest in the group's master tape, you should try to negotiate for 100 percent reimbursement of the group's out-of-pocket expenses, not just studio costs. (Note: the same principle may also apply in contract talks with personal managers and publishers.)

However, the more important reason for keeping tabs on total cash expenditures is to help the group learn fiscal conservation. If one member of the group is going overboard on $20 meals; if another member of the group is making too many long-distance calls; if still another member of the group didn't find out that the printer down the street charged twice as much as the printer across the street would have charged for the same job—it's costing the group money. In time, those meals, telephone calls, excessive print charges, and other "miscellaneous" expenses will run into thousands of dollars. Especially when you're starting out, it's advisable to be very careful with what money you have.

CASH DISBURSEMENTS
(GROUP NAME)

Expense Item	Jan.	Feb.	Mar.	Apr.	May	Jun.	Jul.	Aug.	Sep.	Oct.	Nov.	Dec.
Rehearsal studios												
Equipment rental												
Equipment purchase												
Cartage												
Cab fare												
Gasoline												
Auto repairs												
Demo production costs												
Tape duplication fees												
Attorneys' fees												
Accountants' fees												
Postage												
Office supplies												
Printing												
Telephone												
Meals												
Hotels												
Educational activities												
Publicity												
Insurance												
Office equipment												
Medical												
Bookkeeper												
Rent												
Taxes												
Other												
Other												
Other												

20

Selling Your Body Won't Help (So Don't Do It)

Over the years I have observed hundreds of truly professional music business types. These people are uniformly engaged in the pursuit of money. They are uniformly cognizant of the fact that consumers don't buy records, sheet music, or concert tickets because the lead singer in the group is good in bed—they buy product because it's good music.

Far from acting out erotic fantasies with artists, composers, and producers, most truly professional managers, agents, concert promoters, and publishers don't even consider their clients to be human. If touching is ever necessary, it's either to console the artist ("Hey, forget what the critics said—you were great."), to warn the artist ("If you don't follow my advice I'm going to break every bone in your body."), or to give the artist a routine inspection ("Well, you're halfway through the tour—I'm sending a doctor over to check you out and prescribe more sleeping pills."). People have been known to talk more lovingly to their cars than most music business professionals talk to their human money machines.

Any person who insists on having sex with you before signing a contract is not only a barbarian—that person is also a rank amateur. Many more of these creatures will be found, of course, in the music business jungle than in the legitimate world of major record and publishing companies, where corporate mateswapping has been known to cause severe breakdowns in efficiency.

If you want to sleep with someone, that's one thing, but otherwise you might ask yourself these questions:

"What will I get from going to bed with this person?"

"Probably I'm not the only person who's been propositioned this way. Was going to bed really helpful to any of the others?"

"If I go to bed with this person, won't it change our relationship? Haven't I always felt differently toward a person after having sexual intercourse?"

"Suppose I get a reputation for going to bed on demand—is that so desirable?"

Underscoring these and other questions is my fundamental observation that music business success does not hinge on the performance of physical sex acts. If you're ever tempted to go to bed with a barbarian, take off your stupid cap and start thinking.

21

Be Invited Out of the Jungle, or Get Out Altogether

Time goes by. You've worked hard to perfect your artistry. You think you've made substantial progress in your ability to write songs. You've gained valuable experience playing before audiences. Your friends tell you that a following for the group has emerged, and that it's growing.

That's the way the script should read. The culmination of the story may be that an established A&R producer, personal manager, or publisher hears the group, likes the music, and offers to sign the act. Things may work out this way—then again, they may not. Of one thing I am certain, however: the decision to leave the jungle should never be yours entirely. You should be invited to leave the jungle by a reputable individual or company, or encouraged to leave by an enthusiastic group of diehard fans.

There may be some plausible reasons why a group has not received adequate exposure. The group may not have a business leader, manager, or agent. It may simply be an un-lucky group, a month too early or late to capitalize on a unique opportunity. For whatever reasons, if the jungle isn't working out for you after a year or two, get out. Leave it. There are other avenues for approaching the music busi-ness. You may have failed the jungle exercise, but it may still be too early to say that you lost the war.

Here is what you minimally have when the time comes to cash in your chips. You have experience. You have started to make connections. You have at least earned the right to say, "While other kids were in school learning history, I was in the center of the action, learning where the new music is headed." Quite a few people have been able to parlay their street education into low-level jobs with established, up-town firms.

On the other hand, I don't think it would be fair to give up on the jungle (assuming nothing has happened) without asking some rather painful questions. Why was the exercise unsuccessful? Why didn't it work? Was it the music, lack of money, or a breakdown in communications? Finally, is a music business career truly worth pursuing?

Like many misguided young people, I came out of my own jungle experience realizing that what I thought I wanted to do wasn't right for me. I left owing thousands of dollars, but I was literally a changed person. It was the jun-gle that changed me (for the better, I must say), and for that I will be eternally grateful.

If it works that way for you, consider yourself lucky. The important thing isn't to become an instant success, but rather to learn who you are, what your limitations are, and what you'd really like to do with your life. Voluntarily changing career direction in order to survive and thrive is not a cop-out: it may be the most intelligent decision you ever make.

PART 3

Investment Needs

22

Don't Be a Fool:
Learn How to Raise Money

If you need money to start a professional recording studio, record store, or music business magazine; if your group needs financing to make master tapes, purchase better instruments, or hire a top arranger; if your personal management company wishes to expand its purview into publishing, concerts, and films; if, in order to promote rock concerts, you require advertising, facility rent, and over-head subsidies; if your classical chamber ensemble needs money to finance an international concert tour, showcase in New York City, or commission a new work—for these and other reasons you may be required some day actively to seek investors.

Fund raising is a skill, like anything else. Some people can learn to become expert fund raisers; other people are born with the ability to raise money; still others will never focus on how fairly simple the fund-raising process actually is. I earnestly hope that none of my readers qualify for membership in the third category.

The ordering of chapters in this section should correspond to the orderly progression of steps one takes in assessing, developing, and communicating fund-raising proposals to others. Here, however, are some throw-out recommendations on raising money to get started:

1. Never be afraid to ask.   This is the biggest hang-up for most beginners. God will not punish you if you ask for money. You will lose neither friends nor face if you ask for money properly. What you will most certainly lose, if you don't learn to open your mouth, are the chances for raising money. It's the easiest thing in the world to ask for funding—all you have to do is try.

2. Have something specific to sell.   Potential investors need fast, accurate answers concerning the purposes, objectives, manpower and equipment needs, income, and expense projections for your venture. Until your business plan is well thought out, you are not ready to make telephone calls or write letters.

3. The main thing to sell is experience.   This is the most important thing you have to offer an investor. You know what it's like out there. You've lived the experience. Now you've put two and two together, and you have a specific proposal. It will work for the following reasons (at this point you should begin listing what those reasons are). If, indeed, you are speaking with the Voice of Experience, you will be heard.

4. Form letters are taboo.   Every potential investor should get a customized fund-raising cover letter. Xerox copies of the company's prospectus are fine, but Xeroxed cover letters are a turn-off.

5. Do not mix business with pleasure at first.   Paying back a loan is much more important over the long haul than becoming instant pals with your investor. Getting a check isn't the end—it's the beginning of the fund-raising relationship you want to establish with that angel. Until you are making as much money as the investor, your relationship should be that of servant to master.

23

Choose Business-related Fund-raising Targets Only

In order for there to be even a remote chance of raising money, there must be a mutuality of interests (I prefer calling it the common ground) between the seeker of funds and the provider of funds.

It's not likely, in other words, that a member of the New York Philharmonic's board of directors will want to invest $10,000 in a new rock group, or that a singer who's made millions in rock and roll will suddenly want to start a new career by performing the role of Carmen with the Metropolitan Opera (does this person, we might ask, even know how to read music?).

Investors generally like to get involved in things they feel comfortable with, rather than with polar opposites. It doesn't have to be exactly the same business, but investment seekers would be well advised not to waste time selling the equivalent of meat to a vegetarian, or peddling matching three-piece outfits to members of a nudist colony.

Here are some guidelines to use in deciding where to go for investment capital, depending on the specific nature of your involvement in the music business.

Contemporary pop artists who need better equipment, instruments, costumes, and so on. If you sign a recording contract, the record company might advance money to the group for this purpose (it would be justified internally as an artist development expense); if you do not yet have a recording contract, the money would most likely be obtained from either a personal manager or silent-partner investor.

Record producers who need financing for a master tape. If you have stature in the industry as a person with good ears, you may be able to swing a deal with a major label; otherwise you will have to seek out private investors—preferably one person, although the cost of the tape may require you to form a syndicate of investors.

Promoters who need backing in order to produce a concert. If the act is affiliated with a major record company, the company will pay either most or all of the advertising costs; the rest of the money will have to be raised from private investors.

Classical artists who need money for a showcase concert. This is not a good return-on-investment opportunity (i.e., you will be lucky if you sell fifty tickets; you will be luckier still if those fifty people actually show up). Enter competitions where the prize is a free showcase concert, or contact private foundations interested in music with original programming ideas.

Personal managers interested in expanding into other areas. If just one of your artists is signed to a major label and the product is selling, the record company may finance the entire expansion plan; if this is not the case, you will have to seek funds from private investors.

Persons interested in starting a club.   It may be possible, in time, to finance expansion of a very successful club through commercial bank loans; but beginning club owners will almost certainly have to use a combination of their own money plus private investment capital.

Full-service music publishers.   If you have impressive professional credentials, you may be able to raise money from foreign publishers who will want exclusive licenses to use your songs in their countries. Otherwise, you should use your own money—this is not an expensive business to get into.

Persons interested in starting a recording studio.   If you are a respected producer, you may be able to raise the money from private investors; if not, there is an outside chance in some U.S. cities of getting a commercial bank to lend you the money.

Persons interested in starting an agency.   This business does not require a lot of investment capital (i.e., you don't need an office at first, or a secretary, or fancy furniture—what you do need is at least one marketable artist and the ability to talk endlessly on the telephone). Money to finance expansion of an existing agency will usually come from private investors and/or other agents interested in merging with your firm.

Persons interested in starting a retail record store.   If you have more than a pittance to invest and your business plan is carefully worked out, you may be able to get a loan from a commercial bank.

Persons interested in starting a classical music ensemble.   If you have a considerable amount of artistic stature and a smattering of social graces, you may be able to assemble a group of Ensemble Friends (private individuals, local companies, foundations, arts councils) to help pay the bills. In order to enlist the Ensemble Friends, however, you will have to perform many concerts for little or no pay for at least several years.

Banks (correctly so) don't like to take chances. They will not lend money unless there is adequate collateral, such as cash, purchased equipment, or the money-seeker's home, to secure the loan. Private investors, on the other hand, sometimes relish highly speculative gambles. They may have a real affinity with another gambling type (i.e., the fund raiser), especially if their own money was made in a high-risk field. They may actually gain from losing 100 percent of their investment in a new business if they're in a very high tax bracket. They may also be interested in making new business contacts with people they might otherwise never meet except via the music business entrepreneur's venture.

There is one other very important reason for recommending private investors over any other potential source of capital. Private investors don't decide through committee meetings. Their actions are not restricted by charter guidelines or bylaws. They say either yes or no, but they decide for themselves and they usually decide quickly. Even if the answer is no, it's better to find that out and move on to another investment prospect than to agonize for months over whether the deal you want is going to go through.

24

Narrow Your Focus to Investors in the Market to Invest

There is a tendency for beginning fund raisers to put the cart before the horse—i.e., to allocate most of their time to planning new ventures in minute detail BEFORE ascertaining if anyone is even remotely interested in the venture. My advice is to find out first if there are any potential common ground investors in the market at present. Only after you've made contact with a few likely investors should you go ahead (assuming they're interested) and develop an extensive plan.

There is no official directory of U.S. or international investors with which to begin narrowing down likely investment candidates. Much can be learned, however, by reading the music business trades. Investment bankers, lawyers, and accountants may also be able to provide good leads on who might presently be in the market to invest in your business. Tips may just as easily (less expensively, too, as a rule) be gotten from receptionists, secretaries, friends, and denizens of the music business jungle.

I am, admittedly, a professional fund raiser. That means that whoever I am with, no matter what the circumstances, I am never far from thinking about money. I am always ready to pounce on people who know other people that have a lot of money. Invariably, I ask these questions:

"How well do you know the person?"

"What's the person really like?"

"What's the person doing right now with his time?"

"Do you know if the person has ever invested money before, or if the person has ever made a charitable donation?"

"My project—do you think it might interest your person?"

"How would you advise me to contact the person?"

After that, my procedure is as standard as turning on an ignition switch. Either the person I pounced on (if he still likes me) offers to put in a good word first, or the very next day, while it's still fresh in my mind, I get in touch with the potential investor. I introduce myself as a friend of the person I pounced on. (Note: I will always first get permission from the person acting as a go-between to use his name.) Then I give a brief history of myself, describe my most recent accomplishments, and give a thumbnail sketch of my new business plans.

Depending on whether it's a for-profit or not-for-profit business, I conclude the selling part of the exploratory phone call with one of the following questions:

"Would you be interested in learning more about the venture?"

"Would you like to make an investment?"

"Would you consider making a tax-deductible contribution?"

Seconds later, I know where I stand. Most potential investors aren't interested—that's par for the course. But if a person is interested, it means I'm going to need documentation. It means I'm actually going to have to sit down and formulate a business plan. The point is, there should be a REASON for planning a new business. If no one out there is interested in your idea for a venture, there is not enough reason, in my opinion, to pursue it actively.

25

Match Materials to the Personality of Your Investor

Unless the modus operandi is direct mail solicitation—a tactic used effectively by established nonprofit institutions such as The Metropolitan Museum of Art and the Los Angeles Philharmonic—every fund-raising crusade should be custom tailored to the individual potential investor. Some investors will expect a one hundred–page prospectus. Other investors won't even look at your prospectus; they'll tell you they decided to invest at 2:00 in the morning because they like you and they admire what you're doing (at times such as these, the least you should remember to say is "Thanks"). Either way, it's important to get as much advance knowledge as you can about the idiosyncracies of a potential angel.

There are five basic components to a fund-raising proposal: (1) the cover letter, which summarizes the purposes, objectives, and financial prospects of the contemplated venture; (2) the prospectus, which includes historical background and the actual business plan; (3) public relations endorsements, such as press releases, photographs, chart listings, newspaper stories, sample product, or concert programs; (4) either an audited financial statement or an accountant's income statement and balance sheet for the most recent period of your present company's existence (if you have a company); and (5) a verbal sales pitch that covers the entire scope of your contemplated venture in no more than ten minutes. (Note: Very often when I meet with a potential investor for the first time I ask for five uninterrupted minutes in which to make my case; if I'm talking particularly well that day about my business, almost invariably I walk away with money.)

What one can realistically hope to accomplish by submitting thorough, typewritten, neatly bound *support documentation* is, frankly, not a great deal. If the written materials lend a feeling of seriousness and professionalism to your venture, that is the most that can be expected. But it is wrong to place any major significance on the influence of written business plans on the potential investor. The reason people give money is not because something looks good on paper; people give money because they want to—i.e., they are interested in a specific area, and they need someone with expert qualifications (you) to help translate their vision into working reality.

Let us agree, for the moment, that the fundamental secret to successful fund raising is being in the right place at the right time, and that the value of written materials to the potential investor may actually be negative. This would account for why so many apparently brainless, nonplanning people (albeit with experience) receive funding, while other people, busily perfecting cover letters and sometimes paying outrageous sums to professional fund raisers (not including myself) for this purpose, end up with nothing.

However, the written *business plan* is an absolutely indispensable survival prescription for the fund-raising seeker. A carefully conceived plan should tell whether there is substance or froth to your idea of starting a business. The plan should help bring you within the orbit of potential investors who don't need to be sold on the merits of the plan, but who may desperately need someone to take the idea and run with it. The principal beneficiary of business planning, in other words, is not the fund-raising target; it's you.

Here are some tips to use when the time comes to write down a business plan:

1. Look at your business expenses on a monthly basis. Will you be making more telephone calls, for example, in March than in January? Are you going to need part-time employees in May and June, or are you going to cut back full-time labor in November? Will you be needing an office for the entire year, or for only nine months? Go down your entire list of expense items in this way; it may substantially reduce your total estimated expenditures for the year.

2. Look for the cheapest acceptable way to do things. Most new businesses don't need fancy offices, fancy office furniture, and deluxe office equipment. If you can get by without a postage meter, do it. If you don't really need a paper copier, don't buy one. If you can work out of your home initially, save the money. Keep your expenses down to the bare bone, and maximize net profit.

3. Don't forget to compute taxes. Every employer with employees has to deal minimally with payroll taxes. There may also be duties, levies, freight charges, and other business-related taxes to deal with that are often overlooked by beginning music business entrepreneurs. Find out which taxes are applicable to your business, and factor them into the total expense equation.

4. Add 15 percent to each of your expense estimates. At the end of the year, it's better to show your investor that the business saved money (i.e., your expenses were less than budgeted) rather than that it was forced to reduce net profits. The most expedient way to plan for the unexpected is to formulate an exact estimate of something, then add 15 percent to that figure.

5. *Project income on three different levels.*   There should be a minimum, middle-level, and maximum projected income listing for whatever business you're planning to develop. If, for instance, it's a recording studio, the schedule should reflect billings for partial, normal, and twenty-four-hour use; if it's a concert, the schedule should reflect ticket income based on 50, 75, and 100 percent of tickets sold; if it's an artist investment deal, the schedule should reflect income based on what the artist's debut LP (along with accompanying career development plans) will yield if 10,000 units, 100,000 units, and 500,000 units are sold. Again, these financial projections may not be very significant to the investor. But I think it's an excellent idea for beginning entrepreneurs to work up minimum income projections, subtract income from expense, and periodically ask themselves, "Am I crazy to be doing this?"

26

Make a Firm Offer:
Take It or Leave It

The culmination of the fund-raising campaign—also the last page of the written prospectus—is the making of an offer, otherwise known as "the deal." It is the fund raiser's job to propose the deal. Deals should be based on how much money, time, and professional services a potential investor can be expected to contribute to the new venture. The deal maker should also ascertain whether the potential investor is passionately, enthusiastically, or only mildly interested in the project area.

As I said earlier, some investors would rather seem to lose money for tax purposes than make money. The magic phrase to use when speaking to the former group is the *tax shelter*. Other investors may want to make as much money, and also get as much equity in your business, as you let them. Giving up ownership is personally very distasteful to me. I would rather see beginning entrepreneurs use the following guidelines in formulating their first deals:

1. A corporation will be set up. The fund raiser will not be held personally liable for any debts incurred by the corporation, including the repayment of any loans to the investor in the event that the business goes broke.

2. Stock will be issued in the corporation. The fund raiser will maintain a controlling interest (at least 51 percent) in the corporation's stock.

3. Four-fifths of the investor's financial contribution to the corporation will be treated as a loan. The fund raiser will not have to begin paying back the loan, plus interest (the lowest interest rate allowed by the state), until two calendar years from the start of business have elapsed.

4. The remaining one-fifth of the investor's financial contribution will be treated as equity in the corporation. Depending on the size of the investment, the investor may be entitled to as little as 5 percent or as much as 49 percent of the business. For a 49 percent interest, however, the investor should be contributing at least a six-figure sum to the corporation.

5. The fund raiser will be the chief operating officer of the corporation, as well as the signer of all company checks.

6. The investor will be invited to join the board of directors of the corporation.

7. The investor will have the right to audit the corporation's financial records during normal working hours so long as the investor is a director of the corporation.

The deal should be for slightly more money than you actually need. Some investors like to haggle—initially over price, later over contract points—but most will accept your offer at face value. Having gotten this far, this is hardly the time for you to start acting squeamish. The last card you throw on the table must be a very positive ace: you've done your homework; you have a great idea, and the experience to back it up; you've made the investor a decent offer— now, Mr. Investor, what do you say?

27

Give Yourself a Salary

When money is near at hand, a fund raiser should be in telephone contact with his attorney or business adviser. If the deal goes through, the lawyer will draft a letter of agreement and incorporation papers, as well as attend to any revisions of the letter of agreement following conversation with the investor's lawyer.

Attorneys, accountants, and business advisers should also be used as sounding boards and sources of expert knowledge by the fund raiser. When it comes time to offer a specific tax shelter plan; if you're not sure which way to slant the deal; or if there are legal or tax questions relating to the establishment of the contemplated venture, you will have a need to consult with these professional-services people. You will also, one day, be obliged to pay their fees.

There is nothing troublesome about the legitimacy of having to pay fees for services rendered. What constantly amazes me is how infrequently beginning fund raisers apply the principle to themselves.

Fund raising is an extremely time-consuming job. Many hours will be spent formulating a written business plan. Many, many more hours will be spent on the telephone with potential investors, or in the offices or homes of (let us hope) sure-shot contributors. By itself, the onerous chore of fund raising entitles one to financial remuneration, though perhaps not at the premium rate of $150 an hour, which some lawyers charge. It is advisable, however, to keep track of how many hours you work on a given fund-raising project: beginning fund raisers might value their time at $10 an hour; more advanced fund raisers, who have learned how to compress more work into less time, may figure $25 an hour; and so on.

Even more shocking than the aforementioned is the tendency of most beginning fund raisers to forget to budget themselves a salary as compensation for heading up the proposed venture. No matter if the business is a colossal success or failure, the same principle applies to the fund raiser as it does to the accountant or attorney—i.e., time is money. If you, the fund raiser, are obligating yourself to run a business, you should be paid for your time. (Such payment, incidentally, should be adjusted to include your work in the capacity of professional fund raiser.) You should not have to rely on net income (if there is any) as your sole source of earnings.

I think, however, that too many beginning fund raisers, after budgeting total proposed venture expenses, less salary, lose heart. They are afraid of appearing too greedy, or of having the investor's interest turn sour. These fears, in my experience, are simply not justified if a beginning music business entrepreneur includes a reasonable, subsistence-level salary for himself in the written business plan.

What must be avoided is any appearance that the fund-raiser's control of the expense tiller is less than rock steady.

If you start a potential investor out with a $50,000 capitalization figure, only to come back a week later with an adjusted figure of $62,500, the difference being your salary, you will probably have lost an investor. It is perfectly all right to expect to be paid for your work, but it is poor planning to call attention to this fact after you have already stated your case.

28

Stay Away from Brand-name Institutions until You're Very Big

Reference was made earlier to establishing whether a common ground exists between a person or organization seeking funds, and an organization or private investor able to contribute funds. The common ground mentality works at virtually every level of the fund-raising business. Money will be granted not only on the basis of a solid business plan, but on the basis of race, sexual orientation, religion, age, salesmanship, character, work experience, and personal reputation.

Another very real factor in deciding who gets money is how the contributor of funds slept the night before meeting the seeker of funds—as well as, in today's world, with whom it was that the contributor of funds was sleeping. There are also other factors at work.

Brand-name institutions, such as Bob Dylan, ABC, or the Ford Foundation, are hung up on the glamour of their names. They are unlikely sources of money for beginning music business entrepreneurs. Practically all brand-name institutional money goes to similarly respectable brand-name institutions or brand-name causes, such as the world peace movement, CARE, and Lincoln Center for the Performing Arts.

Private foundations, despite their impressive listing in the Columbia University Press edition of *The Foundation Directory* (every serious classical music fund raiser has a copy), are notoriously bad supporters of unattached, newly formed music organizations. Most private foundations—if they give any money at all to music—support one pet project started years earlier by the organization's founder. Either that, or the foundation supports established, brand-name symphonies and operas, usually the best in town. In panoramic perspective, most private foundations are not interested in funding any music organization that has not already established roots, trunk, foliage, and a women's auxiliary. (Note: This is not to denigrate the need for continued financial assistance of worthy, established cultural institutions. I am merely advising that for organizations getting started, it's going to be difficult to raise money from conservative private foundations.)

If you are a veteran of the armed forces, or if you have been subjected to racial, economic, religious, or sexual discrimination, you may have an effective hook (pardon my crudity) for receiving government funding at the federal, state, and local levels. Then again, you may not. Successful fund raising requires an incredible amount of brute work, for which there is no substitute. If there is an apparent common ground linkage between your venture and an existing program of the federal government, it is certainly worth exploring. But all too often, there are enormous lines asking for U.S. government aid. I frankly cannot recommend government aid as the most likely place—even for veterans—to receive seed money for music business ventures.

Successful fund raising is predicated not just on perceiving the common ground, but on having and applying good common sense. If you're starting up small, think small. Talk to people who can relate to you on more than a business level. Don't bother brand-name institutions until you can show an impressive track record. Above all, put yourself in the other person's shoes: see if the deal, the sales pitch, the purpose of the business, and you yourself appear legitimate. Until you can pass this test, you're not ready to seek funding from major sources.

29

You Are the One
(Who Does All the Work)

There are some other suggestions I'd like to make about fund raising before moving on. In the nonprofit area, it is much better to get ten small grants of $100 each than one large grant of $1,000. New investors are impressed by how many people preceded them to the slaughter, or altar, or however else they refer to the act of writing a check.

Again, for nonprofit seekers of capital, it is advisable to organize an active as well as an honorary board of directors. The honorary board will be a listing of the most prestigious national and local politicians, composers, performers, and arts patrons you can find. Their purpose is to lend legitimacy and prestige to the organization's letterhead. The active board of directors (so-called) includes friends, business associates, the fund raiser's attorney, and perhaps members of the ensemble. Unfortunately, it has been my experience that active boards specialize in being inactive. The only person who can be expected to do all the work at the inception of business is the person who initiated the venture: the fund raiser.

Even in the commercial area, inaction is the rule of thumb. Months may go by before the investor's lawyer and the fund raiser's lawyer have a chance to go over the papers. Unless it is a multimillion dollar deal, the arrangement is not considered important. These are the moments in a young person's life when it is imperative to keep the faith. Don't rely on people to do anything for a long, long time— certainly not until the venture's performance can be evaluated on a budget sheet.

Nobody makes it in a new business without having tremendous personal ambition. Nothing else can sustain the venture during the inevitable lean years. If you do not have ambition—if you're not burning with desire to make a lot of money or get to the top of your profession—you are not cut out to be a private entrepreneur.

But ambition needs to be harnessed. It must be fueled with enough money to support the fund raiser at a bare subsistence level (at least) during the early years. Untempered ambition is folly. Before setting up your own business, please see to it that you are able to survive in the wilderness not for months, but for years.

30

Opportunities Still Exist for Idea People

Recently I had lunch with the operations director of a major U.S. record company with offices in Los Angeles. I was told that the company was expanding rapidly, and that within the next two years at least 500 new employees would be added to the company's Los Angeles labor force.

"Are each of these new employees already accounted for?" I asked, fearing the worst.

The answer was, "Yes, they are." As happens so often in this business, most of the 500 new Los Angeles employees will come from the ranks of the record company's existing labor force. The others will be transfer employees from established record companies, as well as experienced retailers, promoters, producers, and other industry employees who have captured the attention of the company's management hierarchy.

That's how big companies take on personnel. It's 95 percent hiring from within, first from within the company, then from within the industry. The other 5 percent will probably be sons, daughters, nieces, or nephews of the top cadre of managers, along with one or two unattached college reps. Still, there will always be career opportunities for outsiders in the music business—maybe not with major U.S. record companies, but with worthwhile alternatives.

The spark that will most often ignite a rewarding career in the music business in the future will be a great idea married to a common ground investor. More and more, this will be a business governed by cerebral intelligence as well as gut instinct.

The music still has to be in the grooves, but beyond that, so many potential investors have become aware of the staggering profits to be made in the music business that it is today an incredibly bullish market for idea persons. If you are an artist with an idea, a manager with an idea, a record retailer with an idea, a concert promoter or publisher with an idea—if it's really a great deal and it's presented properly, you have a better chance than ever before of getting into the music business as an independent entrepreneur.

The risks are greater than they used to be, but so are the rewards. Idea people are usually the principal officers in the company they help put together. If it is a workable idea and it succeeds, you're in, you've made it, plus you are your own boss. Congratulations!

Big companies are getting bigger. Medium-sized companies can no longer compete with big companies, and are either being acquired or going broke. I have no doubt that the music business will change. It has to, simply because there are so many capable young people who will grow frustrated at the closed-door policy of major companies. Whatever new direction the music business takes, it is a dynamic opportunity for men and women with intelligence, probity, luck, and a hand on the pulse of tomorrow. But take it from me: there's nothing like having your own business. If you can possibly do it that way, I urge you to try.

PART 4

General Business Needs

31

Music Is a Big, Big Business (for What That's Worth)

The purpose of this part of the book is to organize a framework for improving the reader's odds for success when dealing with established personal managers, record companies, producers, publishers, concert promoters, retailers, and special interest groups.

Following this part and part 5, devoted to artists and songwriters, each of the above-named industries will receive individual coverage in parts 6 through 10. But for now, there are enough common ground elements tying these seemingly disparate music industries together for them to be considered as a whole.

The music business is a big, big business. This may not come as a shock to most people. It has been quite a few years now since the record industry usurped the right to be called "the most lucrative area of entertainment" from the television industry. It is common knowledge that the music business is much bigger than the sports business. I am afraid, however, that most beginning music business personnel still do not understand what it means for music to be called— invariably by its own people—a big, big business.

Most industries, frankly, are sensationally overvalued by the media. This is especially true in the case of the music business, which does not yet have a Ralph Nader–type consumer watchdog. No one in the United States knows how many albums are really sold in a given year. No one knows how much money is actually taken in. No one knows whether there is complete racial harmony within the industry, or whether women are getting a square deal. No one knows because no one, curiously enough, really gives a damn.

What this means for professional music business aspirants is very simple. Don't believe everything you hear or read about the industry. The next time you read a trade publication, remember that the lifeblood of that paper, its advertising revenue, comes from legitimate record and publishing companies who expect—and receive—good press. The next time you walk into an office and see twenty-five platinum album awards on the wall, remember that sitting on the board of directors of the prestigious Recording Industry Association of America, the award sponsor, are twenty U.S. record company presidents. Twenty top executives who are in competition with each other but who have a common need to look good, not only in the media but also to prospective artists, songwriters, personal managers, and record producers. According to reliable industry sources, it is really quite appalling how few albums actually merit the distinction of generating sales to U.S. record consumers in excess of one million units, which is what a platinum record is supposed to be.

No doubt I am as ill informed about the truthful condition of the music business as anyone else; however, I am writing for a different purpose and to a different audience than the trades, and can risk being candid. I know that the music business is a big, big business. But many music businesses are failing. Some are on the verge of bankruptcy, including quite a few large, brand-name record companies. I also think there is at least a billion-dollar difference between what the industry says it took in last year (about $3.5 billion) and what it actually took in. When it comes to the music business, I have learned to be very, very skeptical.

Music may soothe the savage breast, but it's also a sucker's paradise. If you're bullish on a music business career, that's fine. Only please be careful. Keep your eyes and ears wide open. Your own lawyer may be guilty of hyping the business. To accept the music business or anybody in it at face value is to be blind, deaf, and foolish.

32

It's the System That Counts

Production. Distribution. Marketing. Sales. Promotion. Publicity. Operations. Accounting. Business Affairs.

These are the words that spell either success or failure in the music business. No matter what size or shape the business takes—whether it's a mammoth record or publishing operation, a one-man personal management company, a small booking agency, a middle-sized independent record distribution firm, or a major public relations house—the applicability of these words is undeniable. These words, which should be memorized, mean BUSINESS.

Let us presume that you are about to leave the music business jungle. How do you know which personal manager, booking agent, or record company to approach? Which record retailer, commercial jingles producer, or concert promoter should you seek employment with? The answer to these and other basic survival questions is to study the company you're looking at in relation to the words listed above. In doing so, you will be performing a *systems analysis* of the company. This is very important, since in business it's the system that counts. It's the company's overall performance level—not the isolated stellar performance of a hot-shot talent scout or mesmerizing company president—that will generate either long-term profitability or unprofitability for you. If you do not comprehend that success in business is a team effort—if you don't appreciate how important it is for each of the nine business areas listed above to be pulling your career forward from the start—then your chances of making money in the music business are minimal.

Let's go through each of the nine terms, define them, and demonstrate their applicability to the most popular music businesses.

Production.   This is the so-called creative department of the music business. Record companies, for example, create master tapes, album covers, 33 1/3 LP's, 45 rpm singles, 8-track cartridges, audio cassettes, and a bevy of specialty products. Publishing companies create songs, demo tapes, and sheet music. Personal managers, through their packaging and artist counseling expertise, help to create careers. Booking agents create an artist roster. Concert promoters produce concerts. Record and commercial jingles producers create master tapes. The record retailer is also a producer: he has produced a store. Artists and songwriters, of course, create music exclusively, They will be omitted from the rest of our preliminary systems analysis story.

Distribution.   This is the network through which the producer of musical goods and services gets his product out into the marketplace. Major record companies distribute product through wholly owned branch sales offices; smaller record companies utilize independent record distributors scattered throughout the country. Major publishing companies distribute sheet music through wholly owned branch sales offices; smaller publishing companies may utilize independent rack distributors, or have a major sheet music distributor (such as Warner Brothers Music) become their sole distribution agent. Ideally, personal managers and agents distribute their product—artists—to record companies, publishers, motion picture producers, television producers, book publishers, and theatrical producers. Concert promoters must develop a distribution network of small, medium, and oversized facilities in which to showcase headline attractions. Record and commercial jingles producers must have access to a number of different record company and advertising agency accounts; the development of these contacts can properly be called the development of a distribution network. As for the record retailer, the profitability of his business depends on how many distribution outlets (i.e., stores) he is able to locate throughout his business area.

Marketing. This is the business planning arm of the music industry. The marketing department of a record or publishing company will decide when, where, and how to release new product, what prices to charge, and under what conditions the product will be entitled to receive additional promotional support. Personal managers and booking agents must formulate marketing plans for each of their artists; these plans will help the manager or agent choose which elements in the total distribution network are right for a particular artist. Concert promoters must design marketing plans for each concert they produce. Record and commercial jingles producers are also concerned about marketing; they will want to know as much as they can about the demographics for a new artist, toothpaste, or scouring pad. Through his own marketing plan, the record retailer must come up with a better idea for displaying product in his store; top-notch marketing savvy will be rewarded through increased consumer purchases, which in turn leads to more favorable wholesale price discounts for the retailer.

Sales. This is the department responsible for selling product. The sales department of a record company services retail stores, international accounts, one-stops (also known as subdistributorships), rackjobbers, record clubs, salvage dealers (who buy by the pound), and eventually budget dealers, after a record has been "cut out" of the first-release catalog of a record company. Publishers sell copyrights to record companies, international licensees, and motion picture, TV, theatrical, and commercial jingles producers; they also sell sheet music to dealers, rackjobbers, and distributors. Personal managers sell artists primarily to record companies, publishers, agents, and motion picture and TV producers. Booking agents usually begin selling artists to concert promoters; in time, however, the booking agent may handle employment opportunities for an artist through the entire spectrum of the entertainment industry, including modeling, posters, T-shirts, books, commercials, and, of course, motion pictures and TV. Record and commercial jingles producers must be able to sell their production talents to the artists they wish to record; afterward, they must be able to sell master tapes or demos to their A&R friends at the record company, or the accounts supervisor of an advertising agency. As for record retailing, the very essence of the business is sales.

Promotion. For our purposes, this means the same thing as advertising. (But note: A large record company will be involved so extensively in promotion that it will create separate departments for advertising—which writes, designs, and places newspaper, magazine, billboard, radio, and TV ads, which the company pays for—and for promotion— which deals with getting free radio play on new record releases.) Publishing companies promote copyrights through airplay and demos; they promote sheet music through newspaper and magazine ads; they promote themselves by advertising in the trades. Personal managers and agents don't usually spend a lot of money on promotion; they get record companies to guarantee tour support (which includes advertising and publicity) for their artists. Concert promoters promote concerts through newspaper ads and radio commercials; they must be very knowledgeable about ways to cut advertising costs, or else, in most markets, they will eventually go bankrupt. The promotional expense bill for record or commercial jingles producers is usually picked up by the outfit that hired them, either a record company or advertising agency. Record retailers promote their stores through heavy newspaper, radio, and TV advertisements; if the retailer sells a lot of records, he may be able to get cooperative advertising support (i.e., the record manufacturer pays most of the cost of promotion).

Publicity. This department is responsible for getting favorable newspaper, magazine, radio, and TV coverage— preferably in feature story or feature interview form. Major record and publishing companies have thieir own in-house publicity staffs. Personal managers, agents, concert promoters, and record and commercial jingles producers usually hire outside public relations firms to work on specific projects. Record retailers normally don't need publicity agents, but they must be careful to avoid negative, or adverse, publicity.

Operations. This department looks after the day-to-day running of the business. Major record companies and agencies have enormous physical plants to monitor, as well as fairly substantial labor forces. Smaller businesses, such as publishing, personal management, concert promotion, and record and commercial jingles companies, may only require a director of operations. However, if the business has a need for inventory control, procurement of supplies, hiring and firing of employees, physical plant maintenance, data processing, and equipment repair, that business will falter, or eventually fold, without adequate operational guidance.

Accounting. This department handles bookkeeping, finance, and payments. Record, publishing, and management companies must keep royalty statements for artists. Agents must keep records of how many concerts an artist presented during an accounting period, how much money the agency collected, and what the agency commission was on those concerts. Concert promoters need to keep accurate financial statements in order to get paid at the conclusion of a concert. Record and commercial jingles producers need to keep accurate accounts so that their employers can see, on an item-by-item basis, why the master tape cost so much to produce. As for record retailers, they must keep an accurate accounting of how many records have been sold, how many bonus records they are entitled to from each manufacturer, and how much their operating expenses are.

Business Affairs. This is the legal department. Everybody needs a lawyer. Everybody hopes to be doing new business, more business, better business. The business affairs department is responsible for negotiating contracts, preparing legal documents for signing, and establishing legal defense of the company's interests. With business affairs, our preliminary exercise in systems analysis comes to a close.

What conclusions can now be drawn?

First, the key to success is distribution. Without an adequate network for selling product—any product—to consumers, the ability of a sponsor company to make money for you is either nonexistent or marginal. When you sit down with a company owner or talent scout, the first question you should ask is, "What is your distribution capability at present: do you have worldwide distribution, national distribution, regional distribution, local distribution, or zero distribution?" If the answer is "We don't have a distribution network yet," and unless there is a very compelling argument (such as a huge cash advance) for hooking up with that firm, you should forget it.

Second, you should be concerned about the operational performance of a company. Of particular importance is the ability of the company to meet deadlines for production, manufacturing, distribution, promotion, and selling of product. The longer it takes for a company to bring out product, the longer it will be before you start to make money.

Third, there is the matter of money for promotion. The best marketing intelligence in the world can't help you develop a career without money. The best record promoter can't get your songs on the radio without support from a national record promotion network, which costs the label a fortune. If the company doesn't have money, it simply cannot compete in today's business with major U.S. companies able to budget millions of promotional dollars for a single new product release. This is the primary reason why so many middle-sized record companies have stopped being independent labels. They are now limited partners (in the trade they're called custom labels) with such multimillion dollar giants as CBS, Warner Brothers, and Polygram Records.

Fourth, which may be the hardest pill for newcomers to swallow, is credibility. Learn never to accept at face value anything you're told about the music business. Forget the platinum albums on the wall of the manager's office. Forget how many pictures of the record company president you've seen in the trades. Forget how delicious your first executive luncheon tasted. This business thrives on hype, which has absolutely nothing to do with reality. If you want to make money in the music business, you must learn to be concerned primarily with seeking the truth.

Fifth, you should be concerned about the number of employees a company has, and the quality of those employees. If selling is required, how many salesmen are there? How many promoters are there? It is highly desirable to meet the company employees and gauge whether they are competent, incompetent, or completely off the wall.

Sixth, you want written assurances that the company will pay you for your services. There will be more about this in the next section, on contracts.

If you take my advice—if you perform a systems analysis of every company that wishes to engage you in business—you will be in for a shock. You will discover that most music businesses are not worth being in business with. You will discover that quite a few companies are incredibly inept, and that still more are on the verge of bankruptcy. What can you do about it? If you want a career in the music business, you're going to have to accept this condition. You may not be able to sign with a blue-chip company at the start. In that case, you have no choice but to grit your teeth, take what you can, and move on to bigger, better-managed, and more profitable companies as soon as possible.

33

Unhappy with Your Contract?
Be Grateful You Have One

How shall we approach the subject of negotiating and sign-ing contracts? Will it be necessary to read this section in church? Shall I stress the fact that this is by far THE MOST IMPORTANT SECTION in the entire book?

No, I shall not. Instead, I shall lead off the discussion with six stark, realistic facts that no one—not you, your lawyer, or your super-duper business manager, if you have one—can change:

1. Until you're a Somebody, you're a Nobody.

2. If you're a Nobody, you really don't matter that much to the music business.

3. If a music business company comes along and offers to sign you to a contract, you should be very, very grateful. Period.

4. If you're just beginning, you have virtually no bargaining position in contract negotiations.

5. Invariably, no matter how many months and how much money you spend on attorneys' fees, the contract you eventually sign as a beginner will be substantially the same document (with slight cosmetic alterations) that was originally sent to you by the company.

6. If you create too much of a fuss over unsatisfactory contract terminology, the company that was initially interested in signing you may lose interest in you completely.

This, then, is a realistic interpretation of the importance of contracts. There's really not that much to talk about at the beginning, although I am tempted to draw an analogy. On one end of a seesaw, high in the air, is a very small child (the professional music business aspirant); on the other end, firmly on the ground, is a very large person (the major company). The very large person does not wish to move; as a result, the seesaw is immobile. In time, however, the very small child does what we hope all children will eventually do: grow. When the child begins to approximate the "heavyweight" stature of the very large person, the seesaw will begin to move. If the child becomes a true heavyweight (i.e., a star), the position of the seesaw may one day be completely reversed. But for starters, there simply is no contest.

What follows is a brief synopsis of the main deal points of music business contracts. It is important to get to know these main deal points, to become comfortable with the language of contracts, and, of course, to be represented by a competent music business attorney. However, it is far more important at the outset of your career to choose the right company (use the systems analysis approach) and to GET INTO BUSINESS rather than be overly concerned about contracts. Once you're in business with a reputable firm— once that company and the rest of the music industry has an opportunity to gauge your fair market value through chart positions, box office gates, or TV ratings—your ability to negotiate better, more profitable deals becomes a distinct possibility.

Contracts between artists and record companies, producers and record companies, artists and agents, artists and personal managers, songwriters and publishers, and manufacturers and distributors have much in common. There are six points to the main deal of all such contracts.

Main-deal point #1 is the exclusivity right, which enables each of the distributing entitites above to represent the artist, producer, songwriter, or manufacturer's product on an exclusive basis throughout the distributor's territory (this can be the world, a portion of the world, or, in the case of an independent record distributor, an isolated metropolitan area) for the term of the contract.

Main-deal point #2 is the term of the contract. Record companies, publishers, managers, and agents usually ask for one firm year of exclusive representation, followed by as many as four one-year option periods that, at their option, they may exercise. The reason used to justify a three-, four-, or five-year contract is the capital investment, often substantial, made by a record company or personal manager to launch the artist's career; in the case of agents, the reason for a long-term contract is to give the agency a chance to generate profits in return for helping an act get off the ground (this usually takes at least two years). Due to the dynamics of the record distribution business, where both parties can gauge how well they've performed for each other after a period of months, not years, the term of a record distribution contract is shorter, and may not even be reduced to writing.

Main-deal point #3 is the out clause for the artist, producer, songwriter, or manufacturer. It is the concept known as mutuality, which when reduced to writing becomes the mutual convenants of the contract. Each side enumerates what it agrees to do during each year of the term of the contract. If one side lives up to its part of the bargain but the other side does not, there may be sufficient grounds (they may have to be proven) for the injured party to breach, or escape, the contract.

If, for example, a personal manager did not use his best effort in trying to get the artist a label deal; if the record company did not release an album guaranteed to be released in the contract, and the album was completed by the artist on time; if an agency entrusted an act to a crooked promoter who ran away with the act's money during intermission; or if a publisher was unable to get a record company to record a songwriter's material—the injured party might complain that a mutual covenant was broken. Unfortunately, it is not so easy to escape a contract for any of these reasons. Publishers will ask for anywhere from two to five years to work a particular copyright. Agencies will argue, "That crooked promoter took the agency's money, too—we'll sue him for both of us," which, in fact, if the suit is filed, may satisfy the agent's obligation to the artist in this circumstance.

Record companies, as a rule, don't schedule guaranteed release dates for beginning artists. Practially every contract contains a notices clause, the essence of which is that the injured party must tell the other party in the contract, in writing, why he feels injured. Then the other party has 30 days usually in which to cure the injury (if, in fact, there actually is an injury).

What may ultimately count is how reasonable the company is with you. If a company sees that an artist is truly unhappy and unable to produce new work, the company may be perfectly willing to sign an unconditional release. Not all companies, to be sure, are run by gentlemen. When in doubt, ask the head of the company during the contract negotiation what will happen if you're unhappy one or two years from now. You might be surprised at the answer you get.

Main-deal point #4 is the right to audit a company's financial statements relating to the business transacted between the parties. This, in my opinion, is an uncontestable point. The only area for negotiation is how long the period for inspecting the company's financial records will be.

Main-deal point #5 is the advance. A single song advance may be as little as $100. Agents and independent record distributors, as a rule, advance nothing. Otherwise, advances are computed as a percentage of total projected sales for a given product. If a personal manager or record company really believes in you, you're going to get a big advance. If a personal manager or record company isn't sure about you, the size of your advance will reflect that fact.

Main-deal point #6 is payments other than advances. Record companies do not make further payments to artists and producers until the company has recovered, or recouped, the total cost of producing a master tape; but assuming that sales soar beyond production costs, the artist and the producer (if it's an independent record producer) will receive a royalty for each record and tape sold for which the company receives payment. Publishers split the income they receive from a song fifty–fifty with the songwriter, except in the case of sheet music sales, where the publisher, like the record company, pays the songwriter a much smaller percentage royalty on each copy of music sold for which the publisher (who pays for the printing) receives payment.

Personal managers establish what their management commission will be for a given artist—these run anywhere from 20 to 50 percent of gross income from all sources—and pay the artist, usually semiannually, the balance. Booking agents charge smaller commissions—usually 10 to 15 percent—although some agents may further reduce the artist's take by charging the artist's account for promotional materials, long-distance telephone calls, and postage. Record distributors merely agree to pay the manufacturer a specified wholesale price for each record that they actually sell. However, since records are not considered sold until they are actually purchased by a consumer, the distributor of slow-moving product often will not pay the manufacturer for many weeks or months. Returns, the product that is not sold, are shipped back to the manufacturer, where they create an accountant's nightmare.

Payment computations can be very tricky. But if you or your attorney think that you're being clever by sitting on a contract for six months while trying to negotiate the rewording of every line, you may be committing business suicide. What counts in business is performance. The longer a contract takes to sign, the longer it takes for the finished product to come out. If the outcome of negotiating a contract is the fostering of mutual hatred and distrust, the exercise will have been a failure. You may have a better contract on paper, but you've lost the affection of the company.

I would much rather see aspiring music business professionals be practical. The most important thing is to be in business. The next most important thing is to turn out the best product you possibly can. If you've selected a good business ally, the money will come, in time. You will be able to negotiate better contracts, in time. By the way, do you know who frequently offers voluntarily to change a deal in favor of the artist or songwriter? It's the artist or songwriter's company. The company doesn't want to lose product to a competitor. They will give you what you want, if you deserve it. That's why I say, "Are you unhappy with your contract? For heaven's sake, be grateful that you have one."

34

Know in Your Heart You're the Best

Whatever it is you want to be, it is essential for you to be supremely confident that you are the best in the field.

Now everyone should know how foolish it is to actually BELIEVE you're the best. Someone is always going to be better at something than you—better at composing, better at singing, better at planning, better at marketing, better in general. The point is to have enough confidence in yourself to persuade other people to believe in you. That process starts from within: you have to be convinced of your own worth before you can expect other people to consider your talents valuable to them.

The music business is one theater where it doesn't pay to be modest. Successful men and women in this business tend to be enormously self-confident. The only way you can possibly get ahead is to come on loud and strong, forcibly, even passionately.

The style one takes to assert his or her dominance in a particular area of the business is a matter for individual interpretation. Some people will want to be more subtle than others. Other people will be prepared to go to extraordinary lengths to show how unique their contribution to the music business can be. However you do it, you must speak up for yourself and your abilities (not even your manager can shoulder 100 percent of this responsibility—you yourself must come across as a dynamic, supercharged personality). The way you do it is extremely important; that's why I think it's so vital for you sincerely to be convinced—even though it may not be entirely true—that you're the best.

This business, which owes so much of its success to hype, needs a shot of egotistical self-confidence from a potential new artist, composer, or executive just for the newcomer to be taken seriously. Then the real test begins. You've convinced yourself you're the best, and you've convinced the other person that you're worth listening to. Make sure that you're ready to be judged. It may be the only chance you ever have.

35

The Timing Has to Be Right

So many people have tripped over their own youthful exuberance. The music business doesn't reward potential artists or employees for their speed in submitting demos or resumes. Contracts and jobs are based, instead, on a single standard: excellence. If your work isn't excellent yet, wouldn't it make sense to perfect it before exposing yourself to ridicule, embarrassment, and a lot of wasted time and effort (and probably expense)?

I don't believe any halfway decent writer—let alone the great masters of composition, theater, or art—would be willing to grant that a published work of his was ever actually completed. Beethoven, had he lived longer, probably would have edited each of his nine symphonies, hoping to make them even better (if that's possible). So many gifted songwriters must secretly yearn for the opportunity to take their hit song back and make it even stronger. The same rule should apply for the novice writer, but very often it doesn't. I think it's fair to say that one of the basic differences between amateur and professional writers is that while professional writers have learned how to be patient, amateur writers, in their haste to become professionals, aren't willing to be patient. It's their loss, and also, in a very real sense, the industry's loss if a gifted amateur doesn't learn the importance of waiting until the song is ready to be evaluated.

Listen very carefully to that song you just wrote. Ask yourself, in your heart of hearts, if it's really complete. Is it perfect? Is it capable of being perfected? Don't you think you should show your best possible side, especially on your first go-round? The people you're going to need behind you are too busy, too inundated wtih superprofessional sounds, to give serious consideration to anyone new unless his work is superextraordinary.

Learn to wait for the best possible moment to submit your material and yourself. The music business isn't going to die overnight. Tomorrow, next week, next year, it's still going to be there, and it's still going to be interested in supertalented new people. So please, be patient.

36

Never Ask Favors

The fastest way to lose potential allies in the music business is to ask favors. It is a very unprofessional thing to do.

Even though most offices in the music business are poorly run, they have at least a semblance of organization and purpose. You can't expect your friend on the inside to jeopardize his or her career by asking the top department person a personal favor. The worst thing that can happen—far worse than the top person saying "I don't do favors"—is for the top department person to grant the favor. Then, if the demo tape turns out to be awful (as is usually the case), the top person thinks less of the employee for wasting his time; the employee resents the friend on the outside who caused him to lose face with the boss; and the friend on the outside discovers that his friend on the inside has suddenly put some distance between their personal relationship.

No matter what the situation—if you have artist demos,

production demos, or a personal resume—the responsibility for getting through to the music business should always rest squarely on your shoulders. Either you're the person who peddles your product around to the different music companies, or your manager does the walking for you. Never, never rely on friends: it's unfair to ask them, and it's the fastest way to turn a friend into an enemy.

One other thing. Never pay a professional to do you a favor. If you hire an attorney or music business consultant to help you, make sure it's for legitimate work rather than the performance of favors. The closer you get to the true power brokers in the music business, the more you realize that these VIP's are even less inclined and less able to do favors than are your friends. Good business sense, not friendship, is the reason that most successful music business tycoons pick up the telephone.

I've always made it a point in dealing with clients to tell them, as soon as the subject comes up, that I can't ask my friends in the business to do anything. Always, things must go through channels. The problem is that I doubt whether every music business consultant is as honest with his clients as I am.

37

Never Deal with an Unreasonable Person

I've already started using the word "reasonable" in this book. It's almost impossible to say what the parameters for a reasonable deal are, since the circumstances and roles of the participants will change from one situation to the next. In essence, though, a reasonable deal is a deal that you personally can live with, and that your lawyer can live with. An unreasonable deal is a deal that you can't live with. The lattitude of reasonable deals may run from 10 to 50 percent of an interest in your gross income each year, but beyond that point, with the exception of special TV mail order or record club arrangements, I would say that the deal is unreasonable.

What the unsuspecting music business aspirant often doesn't realize is that there are other factors besides money that contribute to making a deal reasonable or unreasonable. Much of this had to do with the interpersonal chemistry between you and your business colleagues. Are your colleagues, for instance, going to be easy or rough with you? Are they going to allow you an occasional holiday? Are you going to be able to act as a creative individual from time to time, or are you expected to act like a mindless performing puppet? What happens if you dissent? How much of whatever the total costs are for keeping you in front of the public—including overhead and admininistrative costs—are going to be charged to your account?

A leading personal manager expressed it beautifully: the manager/artist relationship (case in point) is virtually the same as the husband/wife relationship. Both relationships ideally should be based on love and understanding, not the desire for personal gain at the expense of others. It is true that business should always come first in the music business, and, in fact, that in most cases it would be better for business and social relationships to be separate. But the business person should be an honest, decent human being. There should be a genuine feeling of mutual respect and admiration. Short of this, you can expect the members of your business team either to file for divorce eventually, or to make you an exceptionally neurotic person.

38

If You Are an Outsider, You Mean Nothing to the Music Business

Sure, record companies and music publishers listen to demonstration tapes. Personal managers occasionally attend showcase concerts. So do record and concert promoters, agents, and other music business personalities associated with the introduction, or "breaking," of new talent. If you're a complete outsider, though, you mean nothing to this business. Accept it, live with it, and do your best to stop being ignored.

The pressures of being in the music business, if you're really successful, are numbing. People who are tops in the business simply don't have the time to listen seriously to an ingenue—they're too wrapped up in the careers of the stars who catapulted them to seven-figure annual incomes.

They may want to sleep with ingenues, but that's not the same thing as being interested in them for professional reasons. In fact, as far as I'm concerned, going to bed with music business executives in the hope of getting ahead is the most expeditious way to move yourself *out* of the business (see section 20). Executives may hunger for your body, but that's all they'll hunger for. You've compromised yourself. They know that you sold out when the chips were down.

In order to become somebody in the music business, you have to gravitate to an environment where VIP's congregate in large numbers—places like Los Angeles, New York City, San Francisco, Nashville, and Austin. Mail-order discovery is a real long shot, although every so often a group like Boston, which sent an unsolicited demo tape to CBS Records, gets lucky (a little talent doesn't hurt, either).

Once you are inside the environment, you should begin paying your dues. That means, for artists and songwriters, you should be willing to perform in the grungiest smoke-filled cabarets. For aspiring business executives, you should be willing to answer the telephone, type mailing labels, or run errands. Most music business executives have long memories, and a surprising number of artists and executives started out exactly this way. Before you become a member of the club, you first have to be initiated.

39

Use Industry Hangouts for Making Contacts

This is always the $64 question for complete outsiders. If you don't have access to music business insiders, how are you ever going to get the ear of a potential record producer, personal manager, or booking agent?

One of the least expensive ways to meet top people in the music business is by attending educational workshops sponsored by organizations such as ASCAP, BMI, or AGAC. These workshops, which are free, provide excellent opportunities for making contact with professional A&R (talent scout) people from record and publishing companies, as well as with attorneys and, occasionally, personal managers. If you've done your research, you should know which of the ladies or gentlemen on the dais that afternoon or evening is a person who might be interested in you or your music.

Music business educators are also helping to bring top

professionals and aspiring music business employees together (see section 5). Beyond educational opportunities, there is much to be said for tastefully hanging out at record studios and the reception areas of record and publishing companies, personal managers, and agency offices. Notice that these settings are work environments, as opposed to recreational environments, such as clubs or parties. Music business professionals are usually inclined to take it easy when the work day is over. If work is what you're after, make your pitch in a suitable environment. (Of course, if you're an artist, the most suitable environment is a live showcase in a popular cabaret.)

I'm a strong advocate of the personal touch. Get in there, look smart, and sell yourself. If it's done properly, you won't have to wait in line for six months at the personnel department. You'll make direct eye contact with a potential employer, and you will know where you stand with that potential employer within seconds or minutes, not months.

While we're on the subject of person-to-person contacts with music business professionals, learn how to take personal punishment. Learn how to deal with the casual or abusive put-down, and then study what you did to warrant that kind of reaction. When people say "no," they may actually be helping you get your personal act together for the next time you go to bat. Find out what it was that didn't work. Perhaps it was poor timing, a poor choice of words, or maybe you came on too strong at first. These are vital experiences that contribute to your growing and maturing into a person who at least has the semblance of being a together music business employee.

40

Be Wary of Competitions

Competitions, in my opinion, are for losers. If a person goes out of his way to submit a song to the American Song Festival, or a classical pianist enters the Tchaikovsky International Piano Competition in Moscow hoping to become the next Van Cliburn, it's all the same. The really talented people don't need to enter competitions. They have what it takes to build successful careers on their own terms.

The purpose of competitions, allegedly, is to create additional vehicles for exposing talented newcomers to the industry. But what many people fail to realize is that the competition business (no other word describes it so eloquently) cannot afford to be altruistic. The people who develop competitions must put their own self-interest and survival first. As a result, competitions are invariably decided as much by politics as they are by talent. The only people who really win the competition game are the promoters of the competition. The publicity they receive is extraordinary. So is the income generated from international song competitions, which can't possibly be conducted fairly.

Does the reader have any idea how numbing it is to listen to twenty-five different songs—most of them terrible—in an hour? Imagine, then, how callously tens of thousands of demo tapes are taken from their boxes, separated from their checks and application forms, and cringingly placed in the tape recorder. If most songs get past the fifteen-second listening mark, I'd be surprised. The songs that do get listened to for thirty seconds, sixty seconds, or from start to finish, are the exceptional ones. Even if you had an inside lead that guaranteed your winning a competition, I still wouldn't enter—if you're that good the record and publishing companies will want you anyway. (Note: Another reason not to enter, in this case, is that someone might find out one day that the competition was rigged; discrediting the competition winner would be easy.)

As for classical music, I am quite aware that the cream of Juilliard pianists who venture to Moscow for the Tchaikovsky International Piano Competition needn't bother. The one, two, or three top students are signed to major concert management contracts before they leave the United States.

Life itself is a competition. If you're going to compete, why not do it the way most successful people—even children of VIP's—do it? Get out into the real world. As for the artificially concocted competitions, leave them for the turkeys.

41

Think before You Open Your Mouth

You're in a pressure-cooker situation. You've never been involved in a contract negotiation before. You don't know what to say to the record company president. You're actually discussing album concepts with an A&R producer. Your entire life may be riding on whether you say "yes" or "no." Don't you think it would be better to give the matter some thought before you make that critical decision?

You know it would.

Everyone goes through these crisis periods; some people just seem to go through them better than others. The trick is never to be thrown off guard. Find out as much as you can about the people you meet, and never make a snap decision. If you don't understand something, ask to hear the question over again. Give yourself that split-second opportunity (if you think fast) or that evening to sleep on it (if you think slow) before you make your decision. This principle applies not only to momentous decisions but to everyday responses over lunch or coffee.

Reasonable people—i.e., the only people you should ever be involved with in business—will usually encourage individuals just getting started to take their time. The reason for this is not just professional courtesy. Rather, these reasonable people know that success in the music business hinges on the extent to which the parties in a contemplated venture are committed to becoming successful. They would much rather wait for the moment when an artist, for example, says, "I've given it a tremendous amount of thought, and as a result I've decided to go ahead with you." They don't want to wast the artist's time, but, even more to the point, they don't want to waste their own time on a venture conceived halfheartedly, whimsically, or without serious regard for whether the artist really wants to follow through.

Perhaps this is the best way to sum it up: when you're out in the business world, when you're talking about the music business with anyone, consider yourself onstage, performing. The way you look, the way you talk, and especially the things you say are going to tell the other person, group of people, or large assembly something special about you. Don't blow it.

42

Always Be Polite, and Always Ask Questions

It doesn't require a 500-page book to counsel industry prospects on the right way to ask questions, but a few paragraphs on this subject may be most helpful for uninitiated seekers of superstardom.

Some people have never learned the proper way to take "no" for an answer. The usual reactions are a combination of pain, chagrin, unhappiness, and then defensiveness, as in "You're wrong, I'm right," or "You're an idiot—this stuff I wrote is great, only you can't hear it." This may be true in rare cases, but more often than not the person who says no is offering the most important educational opportunity for self-improvement that you'll ever receive.

When a professional A&R person says "Not interested," it's the chance for the enlightened individual to ask the simple question, "Why not—why aren't you interested?" People who can enter into meaningful dialogues about the strengths or weaknesses of their product have an infinitely better chance of succeeding in the music business. Everyone has something to learn. Some people, unfortunately, are less open to learning than others. Some people take things too personally. Believe me, the record industry is one business that is very impersonal. A song is like a slab of beef to an industry professional, nothing more. The only thing that matters is how good the song is, or how good the artist is. If you climbed Mount Everest in order to compose that particular song, it wouldn't matter. The quality of the song counts for everything.

Get into the habit of always being polite with people and always asking questions, if you haven't already. Do it like this:

"Hi, did you listen to my tape yet?"

"What did you think of the material and the way that it was put together?"

"Well, thanks very much for listening. [We shall presume, as is usually the case, that the A&R producer passed on the song.] By the way, would you mind telling me what you didn't like about the music?"

"What *did* you like about my song?"

"Can you recommend any other A&R people to me who might be interested in hearing my work?"

Take notes, if you have to, or get a telephone pick-up and tape the conversation so that you can review it later. Sound very relaxed and laid back, if possible. It's usually better to do this over the telephone—a lot of people feel uncomfortable explaining what they think is wrong about a demo tape when the artist is sitting across from them in an office, ready either to strangle them or break down hysterically.

As for being polite, this is an acknowledgment of the professional courtesy extended by the A&R person in listening to your tape and talking with you. It's also a reminder that you may be returning to that same A&R person with a perfected version of the same song or an altogether new one.

I am not suggesting that you should try and change your compositional style to make an A&R person happy. That's almost impossible to do, anyway. But you can benefit immensely from professional criticism. It's free, it's very much to the point, and it's worked for hundreds of artists who otherwise would still be nowhere.

43

Don't Forget to Say Thanks

This is such a little thing, yet it's probably one of the most important survival tips of all. When a person does something nice for you, say thanks. Either do it in a letter, or call the person up the next day and tell that person how much you appreciated what he or she did. You have no idea what a difference it makes to reciprocate kindness, or how much more esteemed you will be in the minds of industry magnates.

I don't know why the great majority of aspiring music business professionals haven't learned to say thanks. Perhaps they style themselves too busy, or too important. Perhaps they haven't tried composing a letter since the tenth grade. I suppose the basic reason why more people don't write thank-you notes is that they are lazy. Very lazy, and very, very rude.

Writing a nice thank-you note is such a classy thing to do,

especially if you express your appreciation in a simple, genuine way. What's more, a thank-you note stays in your mind. I've taught more than 1,000 students, but the ones I remember the most (including their names) are the students who said "Thanks for the course" in writing.

I write thank-you notes constantly, whenever somebody takes me to lunch, whenever I get a good deal, and whenever someone has contributed something important to my work. Write your thank-you notes in longhand, if your handwriting is legible. And if you've never written a thank-you note, jot one off right now to someone you like. He or she will be glad to hear from you.

44

Don't Do Anything until You're Ready

Getting your act together is the most important success ingredient in planning your music career. Until your product sounds unique, and until your delivery of that product is absolutely professional, you shouldn't do anything to advertise your existence.

The starting point for any meaningful relationship with the established music business, whether you're an artist, composer, or personal manager, is having something to sell that's commercially viable. Brownie points aren't given for how many hours a day you practice, or how many years you've taken to get to where you are. The bottom line today is that you have to EXCEL at what you're doing. If you're that good, you have at least a fighting chance to become successful.

If you're just beginning you should be rehearsing behind closed doors. From deep inside, your Muse must be exposed to intensive self-criticism. Nobody else can do this for you. You may be better off collectively rather than working as an individual, but the people involved with you in getting your act together must be totally into creative music. They must help discover the real "you" (or it it's a group, the real "us"). It's the one situation in the music business where you shouldn't think about the business of music or any other external forces. All that matters is the music.

Some groups put their act together in six months, others in two years, others in five years, others in ten years. Elsewhere in this book (section 35) I suggest that nobody ever actually completes putting his or her act together. If you are in doubt (you should be), I would advise you to be extremely patient.

Somewhere in the midst of this creative process you will sense the dawn of a significant new something. Be very careful: what you think is the right approach may only be a creative quagmire. The best way to test your abilities is also the cheapest way. Turn on the radio and listen, really listen, to what the competition is doing. Then ask yourself, "Am I really there yet? Am I really in that professional league? Is it possible to get a little bit better?"

More and more people seem to think that by studying the music business they're going to learn how to circumvent the need for being supertalented. Don't get your hopes up: it just doesn't happen that way most of the time. Every year the competition gets rougher. Every year the record companies can be more selective than they were last year. Being supertalented is still the primary requisite for any chance at a meaningful career in music. Learning the music business will help you make the right career decisions, but the primary responsibility for having any chance at a potential career rests on your shoulders.

45

Always Get Permission to Use Someone Else's Material

You will save youself a lot of anxiety and potentially valuable connections if you get into the habit of thinking "permissions" at every turn.

If it's not yours, in other words, get permission to use it. Whatever it is, it belongs to somebody else. It is considered stealing to use a copyright or trademark without permission. Under the new copyright law the use may be legally all right, but to the old-line music industry it will always be an infringement to use copyrighted material without at least verbal consent.

Those uninitiated as to what is protected by copyright may be stunned both at how comprehensive the law is, and at how picky copyright owners can be when provoked. The lyrics are protected. Separate lines of lyrics are protected. Groups of words from separate lines of lyrics may be protected. The title of the song normally is not protected, but if someone could prove that a title had been taken from an as yet unpublished song, look out.

If the music is printed upside down so that nobody knows what it is and the clef signs are removed, that still may constitute an infringement. Reprinting from the original score is especially damaging. In short, whether it's words, music, photographs, liner notes, or anything else, you shouldn't be using it without first getting an O.K. from the copyright owner.

The applicability of this advice extends to trademarks as well. For example, a group should not use a name that has already been registered as a trademark or service mark with the U.S. Office of Patents. As soon as records featuring that group are distributed by a major U.S. label, the owner of the trademark in that name can demand that the group's name be changed. This problem can be avoided for about $150 by having a patent attorney handle the filing of a trademark registration form (including a search of existing trademarks) with the Office of Patents in Washington, D.C.

You may never actually be sued for using copyrighted material incorrectly. However, it is important to avoid damaging your relationships with the music business. Don't take chances on losing potential allies. Getting permission is a painless, foolproof way of showing the industry what an honorable business person you can be.

46

For Beginners, the Business Moves at a Snail's Pace

One of the most exasperating experiences beginners go through is waiting for their first contract to be signed. Similarly frustrating business junctures are waiting for the first album to be shipped, waiting for the first major concert tour to take shape, and, perhaps most agonizing of all, waiting for the first royalty check to reach your mailbox.

Don't go crazy if a company offers to sign you and then nothing seems to happen. You must learn to be patient. Until your sales potential can be properly gauged, you really aren't that important to the company. You mean something, otherwise you wouldn't be offered a contract, but just how much you mean must be tempered with the ongoing business of running the company, dealing with the grievances of established artists, and doing whatever else involves guaranteed earnings, as opposed to the long-shot prospects you represent to the A&R department. If you think you'd be treated differently anywhere else as a pure beginner, you're being unrealistic.

Here's an example of what I'm talking about. Let's say that the A&R department votes "Yes, this artist should be signed." It will take several weeks for the business affairs department to draw up the contract. Negotiations involving the artist, the artist's manager, the artist's attorney, and the record company's attorney can now begin. It may take days or weeks to arrange a single telephone conference call. Then the artist's lawyer will prepare a revised contract and send it over to the record company for approval. (Note: The artist's lawyer may also be very busy and consider the artist a low priority client; some artist's lawyers drag their feet even more than record company lawyers.) The record company lawyer will now have to renegotiate the revised contract before sending it on for approval by his boss.

This exercise may take anywhere from three to six months to perform. It may take weeks just to get the necessary signatures on the contract (heaven forbid if more than one record company executive has to sign for the company). The best thing to do during this period of acute anxiety is to concentrate on your work. Try not to think about the contract. It won't do any good to get on your lawyer's nerves or on the record company's nerves. Just be cool (either that, or close all the windows in your car and scream your head off).

Having at last overcome the contract-signing hurdle, there is now the studio production hurdle, followed by the manufacturing, shipping, and record release hurdles. Approximately one year from the release date of the album, the artist may see his first royalty statement and, although there's no guarantee of this, his first royalty check. Well, here's hoping that the artist was able to negotiate a sizable cash advance against record royalties. Considering how slowly this self-proclaimed high-velocity business sometimes moves, he's definitely going to need it.

47

If Dumping Is Inevitable, Come Out of It with Something

It happens every day at all levels of the music business. A new personal manager who brought the artist to the record company is asked to leave. One of the cofounders of a rock group is told to get out. A five-year-old songwriting team breaks up because the lyricist no longer feels compatible with the composer, or vice versa. The person who was promised a record company job waits and waits and waits, but still (probably for political reasons) no job.

Everyone gets dumped on at one time or another. It's a painful trip, usually for both parties. But if dumping is inevitable, for whatever valid or trumped-up reasons, it is better to leave the arrangement—albeit with something—than to try and patch up differences. Being unhappy is not conducive to work, which in turn is not conducive to making money. If acute unhappiness grinds your business to a halt, that is the time to get out.

The best way to protect yourself from getting dumped as, let's say, a personal manager is to have a written agreement with an artist, and a record of cash receipts and time spent developing that artists's career. Short of having something in writing, which you usually won't be able to get because the artist wishes to remain free of contracts, you must be prepared to make a nuisance of yourself with the artist, the record company, and the artist's new personal manager.

If the relationship existed over a period of months or years and you can substantiate that claim, you have strong evidence of a least an implied management services agreement that will probably result in some sort of cash settlement or royalty kiss-off (from the artist's first LP) designed to keep you quiet. You must be prepared to clinch in the corners with these antagonistic forces. You can only afford to do this, however, if you have been completely honorable and aboveboard with the artist. If you yourself have skeletons in the closet relating to the artist, you may be afraid to stand up for your rights.

You WILL be dumped on. Accept it as part of your learning experience. The best way to prevent getting dumped is to select intelligent team members who are truly considerate of your worth and who appreciate your contributions to the team. Unfortunately, there is no guarantee that a considerate team is also a good team. Here's hoping that you choose right on both counts.

48

The Key to Success
(by Now You Should Know)
Is Distribution ·

As a practical matter, this chapter is intended to reinforce observations made in section 32. Regardless of what area of the music business we're talking about—records, publishing, management, agencies, concert promotion, record production, jingles, or retailing—the key to success is not how popular the head man is in the industry, or how much publicity he gets, or how wealthy he is, or what his track record with artists has been in the past. The key to success, in one word, is distribution.

Without the ability to get product into the marketplace, you can have the potentially greatest hit record in the world and nobody will know about it. That's why so many of the smaller labels and publishing companies are hooking up today with major record and publishing companies. Most of the big companies are poorly managed, but at least they have the pipeline for distributing records and the ability to pay on time. The largest of these companies also have a lot of money to fuel that pipeline with advertising campaigns, merchandising blitzes, artist showcases, and a national record promotion staff. Each element of the business system contributes to, and is a function of, distribution.

This same principle applies to the other areas of the music business. Booking agents are only as strong as the network of concert facilities they've been able to develop for their artist clients. Personal managers, to be effective, must be on very close terms with top-level executives throughout the industry. Concert promoters who don't have access to major facilities aren't major concert promoters, because they can't service major pop acts with massive audiences (which, in turn, generate superstar talent fees). Independent record producers need major labels to distribute their records. Without adequate distribution, the independent producer, whose principal source of income is production royalties, will find it difficult not only to build a good reputation, but to survive.

In shopping around for a business team, the principal questions to address are, "How extensive and professional is this company's distribution capability? Can this company get my product exposed in the marketplace? If so, how?" Answers to these questions must be based on the present condition of the company, not past performance.

49

Don't Be Too Uptight about Lawsuits

If we believed everything written or spoken about the music business, it would be hard to imagine any work getting done. Everyone, it seems, would be in court suing the pants off each other, hoping to collect punitive damages, attorneys' fees, or temporary injunctions.

In reality, the bark is much worse than the bite in the music business. Anything that has to do with courtroom litigation or arbitration is not only a pain in the rear, it's also very expensive. Only if it's a major problem involving lots of money, or if the reward for winning a case far exceeds what it costs to prepare and argue the case, will music publishers, record companies, managers, agencies, and artists actually become embroiled in legal actions.

The onus for doing wrongful things in the music business is probably less than it is in most other industries. Very few lawsuits ever make it to court. Nobody wants to get involved in a trial. Among other things, the plaintiff might lose. (Note: Outside New York, Los Angeles, and Nashville, plaintiffs run the added risk of pleading before a judge who may know virtually nothing about the music business. Sometimes even the best lawyer money can buy can't assure a victory for the plaintiff, even if it appears to be an open-and-shut case.)

Don't get the idea after reading this chapter that you can go around pirating songs and phonograph records with impunity. The main defense for being honest in the music business has been, and will continue to be, an individual's personal reputation. If you want to get ahead in the music business, it means that you have to be relatively clean. Not squeaky clean, to be sure, but more clean than dirty.

If, by the way, you ever become involved in a lawsuit, try to settle out of court. The litigation process involves quite a few steps prior to bringing the case to trial. These steps include the lawyer's client interview; pleadings, which list the plaintiff's grievances and demands; motions addressed to pleadings, which are the plaintiff's follow-up to the defendant's response to pleadings; discovery proceedings, which is the accumulating of evidence for both sides; the pretrial conference, where attorneys for both sides meet with the judge; and the pretrial order, where the judge narrows the issues of the case in the presence of the lawyers.

At each of these pretrial junctures, the parties can resolve their differences and reach a settlement. Needless to say, even if the case doesn't make it to court, the lawyers have enough work to keep them busy.

50

Nothing Is Forever
in the Music Business

In this section I have attempted to develop a framework for assessing music business companies on the basis of their true return-on-investment value to individuals just getting started. But what happens, as is usually the case, if on your first go-round in the music business only one company is interested in you, and it's a company without an A-1 performance record?

My advice is to take the job. Get into the industry. Nothing is forever, especially in today's business. Everything is malleable, even contracts. So long as you are in the industry with a product people can react to, you have at least started out, and are in the run for the money.

What happens to exceptional veterans of the music business is exactly the same thing that happens to the most talented newcomers. Inevitably, their careers go forward. Artists will eventually be invited to leave a two-bit record company for a major record company. Songwriters and record producers will eventually be invited to work with major acts. Managers will eventually be invited by major labels to represent some of their newly signed, presently unmanaged acts. The cream of the retailers and distributors, if they haven't already grown too big in their own businesses, will eventually be lured away by major manufacturers, such as CBS or Warner Brothers Records. This pattern for getting ahead has been part of the entertainment picture for thousands of years.

I am not worried about the truly gifted seekers of superstardom. Most people, after all, must PERFORM as part of their job in the industry. It is virtually impossible to keep a dynamite artist under wraps, just as it is to conceal a brilliant manager, agent, or record promoter from the industry for more than a few years. Eventually, everyone in the music business who's good knows everyone else who's good. And I can assure you that the best people, no matter what they agreed to do for their original employer, can find a way to get out of the deal.

On the other hand, I would hate to think that some readers might cancel a decision to get started with a particular company because of a purely literal application of the systems analysis guidelines. These are models, nothing more. In reality, you take what you can for starters, and consider yourself lucky to be playing ball. If you stay healthy, if you're lucky, and if you get that minimum exposure necessary, you may one day step up to the plate and hit a home run.

PART 5

Artist and
Songwriter Needs

51

Start Looking for
a Personal Manager
or Music Publisher First

Finally, after a lengthy gestation period, an artist or a group of artists is ready to approach the legitimate music business. There is a right way and a wrong way to do this, in my opinion. The right way is to go after the most essential elements in career development first and leave the other parts of the total music business for later. In this business, if you get to first base with the right person, you have a very good chance of rounding the bases and scoring.

The most essential music business element for an artist is an established personal manager. The most essential music business element for a songwriter is a music publisher. If you're a singer-songwriter, I'd rather see you go to a personal manager first, although the manager of your choice might give you such a runaround that you have no alternative but to expose your material first to a publisher. A well-connected personal manager, however, will be able to open more doors for you than any other individual in the music business.

The reason you should go to a personal manager first is because the manager is more inclined than the publisher to visualize you as a total entertainment phenomenon. Unlike the agent, who has a specialized interest in concerts for new artists; unlike the record company, whose primary business is selling records; unlike the music publisher, whose primary business is selling copyrights—the primary business of a personal manager is to develop an artist's career in all areas. Personal managers are usually closer to the artist than any other participants in the industry. If an established personal manager joins your business team, you will be working with a person who not only can visualize long-term situations, but who has the connections to get your imaginative ideas off the ground.

The manager's incentive—between 20 and 50 percent of the artist's gross income each year—coupled with the reality that time is of the essence (i.e., the personal manager is committing his valuable time to you, for which he would like, one day, to be paid) makes it that much more probable that the manager will take the career of a new artist signed to him very seriously. If, however, the artist's first series of records flops, the artist will more than likely be jettisoned from the personal manager's talent roster.

The difficult part, of course, is getting the attention of top managers. The bigger they are, the less inclined they seem to be to listen to new artists. I would recommend approaching several leading managers at the same time, but I would pay particular attention to the personal managers who are just beginning to surface in the trades as subjects for interviews. These managers, who are definitely on the way up, may still be willing to listen to new material. Even so, you will have to be very persistent, patient, and extremely lucky to get an audience with any established manager.

I must tell you how some of the leading personal managers conduct business. Their schedules are crazy. Their secretaries are crazy. The phone calls never stop coming in. Everybody wants a piece of the manager's action. And very often, right in the midst of this incredible maze of confusion, you find the Wonder Boy, the personal manager, reading a comic book or watching television or, just for that period of time (an hour, a half-hour), being available for new ideas.

Luck occasionally conspires to place a talented artist in the lobby of a personal manager's office when the manager has free time and a willingness to say "Hi" to somebody new. So it may be quite true: the difference between you and Peter Frampton, John Travolta, or Peter Townshend may have absolutely nothing to do with their being more or less talented than you. It may well hinge on a canceled appointment, a boring day, or a chance meeting in the elevator, restaurant, or men's room with a genius-type personal manager.

52

What to Say at Your First Meeting with a Personal Manager

The characters will change, but, basically, during your first meeting with a personal manager you should do six things:

1. You will thank the manager for agreeing to meet with you.

2. You will tell the manager briefly how you got to where you are: the history of your group, where you've played, and what your audiences have been like. This history should take less than a minute and a half to communicate.

3. You will summarize for the manager where your group's collective head is right now with regard to its preferred musical style, mode of performance, instrumentation, group size, and so on.

4. You will tell the manager what you think makes your group unique—this should take less than thirty seconds, and you will look the manager straight in the eye when you say it and sound totally believable.

5. You will inform the manager that you are not a dummy, that you realize your job is primarily to create music, and that you appreciate the manager's inclination to be creative in his own right.

6. You will thank the personal manager for letting you speak without interruption for approximately four minutes. Now you are eager to hear what the manager has to say concerning your group and its chances for success.

That's the way it should be done. Most new artists, however, come off sounding like fools when they speak to a potential manager. The uppermost question in the artist's mind usually is "How much money can you make for me, and how much of it are you going to pocket for yourself?" It is a big mistake to start talking about money before establishing whether there is any other potential basis for developing an artist–manager relationship.

As I'm writing this, I'm thinking of how certain leading managers that I know would conduct this initial, crucial meeting. Consciously or otherwise, each would want to establish his power over the artist. They might not allow the artist to make an opening presentation. Most of them would hang their egos out for some intense "I-am-the-greatest" chest beating. They would be glad to have someone in their presence who would not talk back to them for a change— who would let them go on and on, usually about nothing relating to the meeting at hand. Take it in stride, artist: it's just the beginning.

Most personal managers will already have decided to take the artist on before granting the meeting. What they're interested in finding out is what the artist is like away from his music. Is the artist intelligent, for instance, or is he a jerk? Can the artist be bullied, or is he capable of taking direction? Artists, in turn, should be sizing up the personal manager both as a human being and as a business mentality. When you're in the presence of a brilliant personal manager, I can assure you that you will know it instantly.

Both participants should act as normal as possible during the meeting. It's merely a test. The first meeting should be concluded with an invitation to hear the artist perform live at the artist's showcase facility, in the hope that this live audition will create enough interest on the part of the personal manager to schedule a second meeting.

53

Get to Know the Personal Manager before Signing a Contract

Something is wrong if the artist and manager don't have at least four substantial meetings prior to signing. There should be detailed exchanges dealing with the scope of the artist's creative potential; the artist's catalogue of songs and demo tapes; whether or not the artist is satisfied with his backup players; what the artist needs in terms of new equipment or instruments that would make him happy; what the manager plans to do; the manager's timetable for the artist; the extent to which the personal manager will be involved in developing the artist's career on a day-to-day basis; whether the artist and manager are able to get along with each other; and finally, what the deal will be between the artist and his personal manager.

Communications should always be person-to-person prior to signing with a manager. Only naive artists are foolish enough to sign with a manager on a blind basis. If you're an artist you may very well be desperate, but don't commit yourself to anyone until you first know whether you can depend on that person to do things, whether the person appears to be honest, and whether the person appears to have a lot on the ball.

As an artist, you'll want to observe how punctual the manager is, or whether he was courteous enough to call you before canceling an appointment. If it's an established firm, you'll probably start meeting other people in the organization: managerial assistants, publicity coordinators, secretaries, and bookkeepers. The question should be raised, "After I sign with your company, who's actually going to handle my career, you (the manager) or your secretary?" If the top person in that firm isn't going to work with you personally from the beginning, I'd recommend that you not sign. You must get top executive service from a management company. Anything short of that and you'll almost certainly get lost in the shuffle.

Do not sign with a personal manager who doesn't first offer you at least a thumbnail sketch of what he's planning to do to launch your career. The manager should give you a strong indication that he's already begun thinking about how to get your career off the ground. Managers who insist on being tight-lipped prior to signing are either paranoid or rank amateurs—either reason, I think, is sufficient for not signing.

Finally, there is the deal. If you're talking to an established personal manager or an up-and-coming manager, there's nothing much to argue. It's take it or leave it (make sure you take it, if you're impressed with the guy). One way or the other, the manager is going to get a good chunk of money out of you. Some managers will keep their percentage down to 20 percent, the industry standard, but charge the artist for every conceivable expense item the manager incurs relating to the artist's career. (Expenses include first-class air transportation, first-class hotel accommodations,

first-class meals, long-distance telephone calls that can easily total more than a thousand dollars a month, demo costs,
promotional consideratons, and accounting services.)

Other managers charge higher percentages but absorb
the artist's expenses. The really big managers may have re-
ciprocal deals with an artist such that the manager gets 50
percent of the artist's gross annual income plus expenses, but
in return the artist gets a 50 percent interest in the personal
manager's entire remaining operation. Those are the parameters of artist–manager deals in today's music business.

If it all seems excessive to you, then consider this. The artist may appear to be sacrificing a lot of money, but the business is so competitive today that established personal managers are literally compelled to live up to their artist contracts. No leading manager can afford having his reputation
tarnished for failing to pay his artist on time, or for
cheating. Besides, it is far better to get a large percentage of
tangible income than to own 100 percent of nothing. If
you're with a major personal manager, you will definitely
have excellent prospects for becoming—even as a 50 percent
partner—exceedingly rich.

The best way for beginning artists to look at money in
terms of personal management is not to look at it at all. If
you're really talented, if you're signed to a major management firm, and if you have any kind of good luck, the
money is going to come. It has to. The most important thing
at the start of your career is to have an opportunity to make
money. Talking back to a top manager because you think
the deal is unfair is the quickest way to terminate that
golden opportunity.

54

What to Do if You Can't Get an Established Manager

If you can't get an established manager, you should try locating a brilliant, dedicated, very hungry unestablished personal manager. New York and Los Angeles are teeming with young men and women who want to manage new groups. Put an ad in the *Village Voice* (New York) or the *Music Connection* (Los Angeles), hang out at NYU or UCLA, ask around, and start meeting prospective candidates. The hope is that you'll find somebody who knows what to do.

Students are always asking me to become their manager. Not interested, I tell them, because I don't have the time. That's perhaps the most decisive question to ask a prospective unestablished manager: "How much time are you going to devote to our group?" Follow it up with this question: "If you're planning to spend a lot of time, can you afford not being paid for months or years to come?" You will discover that the great majority of the applicants who answered your ad no longer fit your basic requirements: unlimited time to promote your group, and the ability of the manager to support himself independently for many years.

Next, you want to ask the remaining one or two applicants, "What will be the scope of your management services?" Listen carefully to the answer. If the prospective manager suggests that it be a team effort involving himself and the group, he's not the right person. If the prospective manager suggests that he doesn't have all the answers, he's not the right person, either. Nobody has all the answers, but any manager who doesn't think he's figured out how to develop an aritst's career isn't worth a dime.

If the prospective manager asks for money from the group, he's definitely not the right person. The person you want must be totally self-sufficient, extremely intelligent, bubbling over with ideas and plans for the group, and yet, at the same, controlled, precise, able to focus on one idea at a time, and able to articulate that idea to the group and to other people.

Other questions do not need to be asked. You can see what the management candidate looks like and how animated he is. You can hear whether he's a natural-born salesman, comedian, or idiot. You can tell whether he's cooking with ideas or whether he's just dreaming. You will discover whether you like this person, whether you can talk to the person with confidence, and whether the potential manager feels the same way about your group.

The question most artists consider important—i.e., how many top people in the industry does the potential manager know—really isn't that important. Talented personal managers always find some way to get through. Your manager might come from a career selling shoes or pumping gas—it really doesn't matter. What does matter is for the manager to have an incredible entrepreneural presence and flair.

The right person will be someone of long-term potential value to you. It is unfair to think, "We'll let this guy kill himself for us, but when we get our first serious contract offer from a record company we'll dump him." If I were the manager, I would insist on a minimum three-year deal with two one-year options at 25 percent commission plus expenses. My argument to the group would be: (1) it's going to take two years to get you a recording contract and your first album release; (2) during that time I'm going to make nothing for working my tail off for you; (3) when you do get your chance, I want to make sure that I'm still around. The artist may argue for an escape clause if nothing happens within a year, but if I were the manager I wouldn't agree to this. One year isn't enough time, when you consider how slowly the record companies and booking agents tend to move.

The final question the artist should ask is "How many other acts are you going to manage?" The answer should be one or two additional acts at the most. Anything more than this and the manager can't do his job properly. Also, the manager should not be involved in other time-consuming businesses, such as records, publishing, or concert promotion.

If you find someone who satisfies these requirements, you've got yourself an unestablished personal manager. If you don't find anyone with these requirements, keep trying and don't do anything foolish. When it comes time to sign with a manager, make sure it's with someone good.

55

Total Artist Development Means Total Financial Participation with a Personal Manager

A personal manager may be within his rights to ask for a commission on his artist's publishing income, provided he is instrumental in deciding how the artist's songs should be packaged and sold. In other words, if the manager takes your raw collection of songs, helps you find an identifying hook, and uses his own sales pitch to get the songs recorded, either by you or some other artist, the personal manager is entitled to a percentage of his artist-songwriter's publishing income.

Why should a personal manager, whose role is apparently self-limiting, get a share of the artist's publishing money? Why do some personal managers, beyond publishing, also insist on becoming the artist's record producer, even if they are producers in name only (i.e., they have no previous production experience and don't know how to produce records)? It's all part of the ball of wax called Total Artist Development. Whatever the manager does to encourage his artist to keep writing, producing, and performing—even if it's just an occasional vote of confidence—is valuable consideration, if without this support the artist would become unproductive.

Some managers are much more involved in creative planning than others, but the underlying principle is the same. The artist must be willing to concede (if it's true) that his total talent spectrum was influenced, either one element at a time or in an explosive burst of self-realization, by the manager. If performing leads to composing, which in turn leads to producing and directing, the manager may be absolutely correct in saying "I was responsible for this growth. I gave the artist confidence when he needed it the most. Therefore, I am entitled to whatever financial interest is considered reasonable by industry standards in all areas of the artist's subsequent career that germinated from my initial contribution to the artist."

Reasonable participation by a personal manager in an artist's career most often takes the shape not only of a management contract but also a copublishing deal, where the manager receives one-half of the publishing half of the business, or 25 percent (the writer's half of publishing income, which is a separate 50 percent, is kept by the artist). If the manager has the time to get involved in record production and the artist does not object, a separate production deal may be drawn up, or the manager may be able to parlay a custom-label deal with himself as a substantial stockholder. There may also be a separate contract governing the artist's souvenir and T-shirt merchandising business.

If you are totally unattached when presenting yourself to a manager, you should expect more than a management contract today. Don't take offense: it's a legitimate request for the manager to make, provided he does the work.

56

Say No to Working on a Handshake in the Legitimate Music Business

Some artists will insist that the only way they can work with an unestablished manager is on a handshake. Some managers, on the other hand, as an inducement to secure artists will offer to work on a handshake. In both cases, I would be highly suspicious of the offer and would not accept it. (Note: Section 6 specifically advises beginners not to sign binding written contracts. Once inside the legitimate music business, however, it is always better to work with written agreements.)

Personal managers who don't insist on a written contract, in my opinion, are evidencing a considerable amount of naivete about the business. They don't realize what colossal circumstances may intrude on their relationship with the artist: the big-time management competitor who may come along; the multimillion-dollar record company offer, contingent on the artist's signing a management contract with the president of the record company; or the aging bass player in the group, tired of performing, who has decided to assume managerial control. These things can happen. Protect yourself by putting it in writing.

Artists should protect themselves, too. It's much easier to get out of a contract if the manager's services are specified in writing and he doesn't live up to them. If, for example, the personal manager agrees to exert his best efforts to obtain a recording contract, and the group can prove that the manager did not exert his best efforts, there will be no contest when the group asks to leave. Without the contract, it's the group's word against the manager's work, and it's not as easy to argue what both parties allegedly agreed to do (the mutual covenants) for each other.

Let it be a competency test for the personal manager to have a contract drawn up, pay for it, and give the artist plenty of time to read it over before signing. Even with an unestablished, knowledgeable personal manager, there should be little room for negotiation. Think it over, but if the manager appears solid and there are no other potential buyers, sign.

57

Stay Away from Business Managers While You're Getting Started

Business managers are a mistake for beginning artists. Usually the business manager is a lawyer who acts as an administrator of a successful artist's personal and business affairs, including investments, property upkeep, and the negotiating of deals. Business managers are either paid a salary by the artist or given percentage points (up to 10 percent) of the artist's annual income. But the business manager is not a substitute for a personal manager. If you're just getting started, you need personal management service. You need somebody to go out and hustle for you day after day. Most business managers are very capable people, but their superstar clients afford them the luxury of working out of their offices and waiting for the telephone to ring.

Nobody is better equipped to assist an artist than an imaginative, available personal manager. The manager's job is to develop the artist's career and to get the artist some business. The manager will eat with the group, sleep with the group (literally or in the figurative sense), and, above every other consideration, give the group what it probably needs the most: confidence. The group must pay careful attention to selecting the best possible management candidate, but after the decision has been made the group should return to their music and let the manager have a chance to do his thing.

58

Select a Publisher That Can Distribute Your Songs

Songwriters must first learn to differentiate between the various types of music publishing entities. A full-service independent publishing company, such as Chappell Music or Famous Music, handles copyrights assigned to it on a worldwide basis. Independent publishing companies take a very aggressive stance on promoting newly acquired copyrights to major domestic entertainment users, such as record companies, motion picture, TV, and theatrical producers, as well as international users of songs.

A publishing company affiliated with a record company, such as April/Blackwood Music (CBS) or Jobete Music (Motown), is similarly equipped to handle both the worldwide utilization of songs, and the worldwide collection of publishing income. However, an affiliated publishing company may limit its copyrights either to songs either already recorded on a sister label, or to songs that were assigned to the publishing company as part of the singer–songwriter recording agreement.

Some of the most successful publishing companies are known in the trade as desk-drawer publishing firms. These companies, such as Charing Cross Music (Paul Simon) or Magicland Music (Ted Nugent), represent their creator's copyrights exclusively, and are administered by larger publishing entities—either record company–affiliated publishers or independent firms—that have the resources to maximize the desk-drawer publisher's income from writing songs.

The largest percentage of U.S. music publishers are the least desirable firms for beginning songwriters to deal with. They are known as either vanity press publishing entities, or DBA (Doing Business As) firms. Unfortunately, most DBA firms are utterly unattached—by virtue of their copyrights, which no legitimate publisher is willing to touch—to the distribution network required to make a decent living as a professional songwriter.

What makes music publishing even more confusing is that virtually every independent publishing firm is owned by an entertainment conglomerate that is also heavily involved with record companies (e.g., Chappell is owned by Polygram; Famous is owned by Gulf & Western). Also, some record company–affiliated publishers, such as Mighty Three Music (Philadelphia International Records) and Midsong Music (Midland International Records) are more adventuresome than other record company–affiliated publishers, and will acquire songs in the hope that their copyrights will be recorded by labels in addition to the sister record company. Here, then, are some guidelines for ordering the publishing business so as to make money as a professional songwriter:

1. *Select full-service publishers with worldwide distribution capabilities.*   Go right to the source of publishing income. Avoid middle-man relationships with desk-drawer firms

or—even worse—DBA firms. If the publisher doesn't have the ability to promote your songs on a worldwide basis and get paid for the use of your songs (from this income the songwriter receives 50 percent), he is not the right publisher for you.

2. *Use the telephone properly.*   Before submitting demonstration tapes in person or by mail, make a preliminary phone call. Ask if the company is still in the publishing business. Ask if the company is interested in evaluating songs from unattached songwriters. Ask who the contact person is at the publishing firm. Ask to speak to this person over the telephone—if you get through, briefly describe the song (don't sing the lyrics unless you're requested) and ask for an over-the-telephone reaction. The purpose of this exercise is not to promote wishful thinking, but to get substantive answers as to whether there is even any interest on the part of this particular publishing firm in hearing your song.

3. *Don't say that you have a publishing company, or that you're thinking of starting one.* Unattached songwriters with DBA firms are advertising FAILURE when they finally contact the established publishing community. Yet, it is very easy and relatively inexpensive to set up one's own DBA publishing entity today. The DBA form can be purchased at a stationery store. Filling in the form, having it notarized, and registering the form with the department of local city government in charge of new businesses can be done by a person with a child's mentality. But successful music publishers aren't children. They are in business to make money, and their principal livelihood is their 50 percent interest (as publisher) in the songwriter's copyright.

Flaunting one's own publishing company in the absence of a respectable track record is not only a futile gesture—it's downright insane. DBA publisher-songwriters who write good songs and wish to make money will be told, in no uncertain terms, either to give up the DBA publishing concept or to find another legitimate music publisher. Fifty–fifty is an acceptable deal to a full-service publisher; 70–30 or 85–15 (i.e., 85 percent to the DBA publisher-songwriter) is not, unless you are an acknowledged major recording artist. Please, don't choke over your own greed.

4. Song plugging is the key.   The heart of a music publisher's distribution network is the song-plugging department. Without the manpower to get demos listened to throughout the world—without the contacts to get through to major artists, record companies, motion picture, theatre, TV, and international users of songs—the songwriter's income from songwriting may consist of a one-time advanced payment. Again, you may want specific answers to your questions. Who are the song pluggers, and what are their connections? Who specifically does the publisher think might want to use the song? Is there any guaranteed use of the song that the publisher can offer you? If the publisher does offer a guarantee, make sure it is reduced to writing in the contract you should sign.

5. Don't overlook new music publishers.   Successful song plugging can be attributed as much to superior hustling as to the merits of the song proper. Talented new music publishers may be hungrier than main-line established firms. They may have as many worldwide distribution connections as the fifty-year-old firm. If they are affiliated with ASCAP, BMI, SESAC, and the Harry Fox Agency, they may also have the same ability as the fifty-year-old firm to get the songwriter his money. If the beginning publisher really applies himself, he may get a faster response and a better deal for the songwriter than a conservative, main-line publishing firm.

59

What to Say at Your First Meeting with a Music Publisher

You sent your tape to the publisher of your choice. Ten days after you dropped it off, you contact the publisher, find out that he's interested, and schedule a meeting. Here's what to expect in your first person-to-person exchange with a music publisher:

First, you will be given a routine tour of the music publisher's offices. This ritual is peculiar, for some reason not yet explained to me, to the publishing community. Be nice to everybody, remember as many names as you can, and compliment the publisher for having such a terrific staff.

Second, you will be told that either one, two, or all the songs that you submitted on the demo tape are of interest to the publisher. The songwriter should ask, "Exactly what interests you, and how do you plan to go about exploiting the song?" The publisher's game plan should include precise information on professional recording studio demo costs, music business contacts, the publisher's success-failure ratio of plugging songs with those contacts, and an approximate timetable for getting the song(s) released on a major label. Primarily on the strength of this game plan, the songwriter should either decide to sign with the publisher, or pass.

Third, the publisher will produce what looks to be a standard single-song publishing contract (actually, no such standard contract exists). Single-song contracts are usually printed in very small type on a single legal-sized sheet of paper. The publisher may go over some of the terms of the agreement with you in the office. He will ask, "Do you have any questions?" Your answer should be, "Let me go over the contract with my lawyer. If either of us has any questions, we'll get back to you." Then the meeting should be adjourned.

Preliminary meetings are not intended for the publisher to dazzle a potential songwriter client. They are an opportunity for both sides to feel each other out. Some songwriters will discover, for example, that the publisher is not interested in the work actually submitted. Instead, the publisher may be impressed with a songwriter's ability to write lyrics, or with a demonstrated melodic flair for writing disco, R&B, or country music. If, however, a publisher were to say, "I'd like you to try writing an original song with one of our resident people," work on this composition should not be undertaken without a written understanding that would establish who owns what (see section 8). This agreement should be signed by the publisher, yourself, and any collaborators you work with.

Songwriters, in turn, should be able to get a feel for how competent a music publisher is. Most of the major music publishers that I know are soft-spoken individuals. They hardly ever brag. They play their cards close to the table, and they will guarantee the songwriter nothing. Reputable publishing firms do not steal songs; in fact, most major publishers today do not even accept unsolicited demo tapes sent to them through the mail. Also, I have found most music-publishing presidents to be extremely fair when it comes to reverting copyrights back to the songwriter. Major U.S. publishers may not be generous with their money, but the biggest of them are honest.

60

If You Write Hit Songs, You Will Be Paid Handsomely

I have already stated my views (see section 33) on the ineffi-
cacy of trying to negotiate contracts if you're a newcomer. I
find, however, that songwriters especially need to be re-
minded that any legitimate publisher offering them a contract is doing them a very big favor. Until your songs have
established their true value where it really counts—on the
charts and at the cash register—you must be prepared for
the publisher to stand firm on the single-song publishing
contract he offers you.

This opinion, unfortunately, is not shared by the American Guild of Authors and Composers (AGAC), an association of songwriters whose members are entitled to use
AGAC's version of what a single-song publishing contract
should be. Many major publishers, frankly, will not sign
AGAC contracts. The principal feature of the AGAC contract—that the songwriter gets his song back in a year if the

publisher has not obtained a record release or paid the song-writer $250—is particularly offensive to legitimate music publishers. One former president of a major firm told me that he would never work with AGAC contracts because it was "like negotiating with a gun at your head." Other major presidents are extremely resentful of what AGAC's very existence implies: namely, that all publishers are not to be trusted.

AGAC must be seen in historical perspective. Back in the '30s and '40s, when it was called the Songwriters Protective Association, it helped songwriters increase their share of publishing income from roughly 30 to 50 percent in each area of the business except print music. Every U.S. song-writer should be grateful for AGAC's lobbying accomplishments. But AGAC also breeds acute paranoia in many songwriters. It has the AGAC contract. It offers other services designed supposedly to protect the songwriter and his songs from publishers. I find this advocacy of songwriter-publisher adversarial relationships quite injurious when applied to the real world. If you wave the AGAC red flag in the wrong faces, you are likely to be booted out the door of the legitimate publishing community.

Every contractual relationship starts out as a gamble. No one knows what actually is going to happen until it does happen. The odds are, though, that an established publishing firm with worldwide distribution capabilities is going to have a better chance at succeeding than a brand-new music publishing firm, even one that accepts the AGAC contract. And on that note I can speak with some assurance: if you write hit songs, you will be able eventually to write your own ticket. No publisher is going to jeopardize losing you to a competing firm. You will be paid large cash advances, plus you will receive songwriter royalties. If you earn it and you're lucky, the contract will one day read just the way you want it to. But until then, be grateful for the opportunity a major publisher gives you to expose your songs.

61

How to Approach a Record Company

Artists with a unique musical sound are always of great interest to record companies. Here's what to do in order to capitalize on that unique sound.

1. Have the right attitude.   Until you're a superstar, you shouldn't act like a superstar. Act like a professional artist, instead. Professional artists deliver master tapes on time. They take direction from the record company's A&R staff and the company's hand-picked record producer. They are courteous and respectful when talking to record company executives. They are willing to make sacrifices in order to help sell product. They know their place, and they don't make excessive demands.

2. Don't be greedy.   If a record company expresses interest in an artist's demo tape, don't start thinking about six-figure advances. The brunt of record company dollars will initially be spent on production, manufacturing, and promotional costs for the artist's first release. These costs may exceed $250,000 per album for each new artist signed to a major label. Most of this money may never be recouped, if the album is a stiff. Management at the record company knows this; now you know it. On the subject of initial advances, artists should be prepared to receive a bare subsistence income.

3. Have a business representative.   Potential superstars do not have time to handle their personal business affairs. Their job is to compose, rehearse, record, perform, and perfect their musical talents. Record companies are highly encouraged when unknown artists come to them under the aegis of established managers, whose job includes managing the artist's business affairs. If you can interest a leading personal manager first, you are virtually assured of a recording contract in today's business.

4. Deal with full-service companies.   Producing master tapes isn't the conclusion of the record business; it's only the beginning. Every new record release puts the artist's career on the line. If you sign with an independent record producer, a custom label, a new label, or a major label, make sure the arrangement is a full-service deal. Make sure that the record producer has access to a national or international distribution pipeline, and that the artist can contribute postproduction input in the manufacturing and marketing areas. Short of this, with each new release the artist will be playing Russian roulette.

5. Be careful playing the field.   Most record companies take considerable pride in discovering artists. They get quite perturbed if an artist decides subsequently to try his luck at other companies before signing a record contract. If you want to play the field, first tell the record company that discovered you what you're planning to do. Do this as a courtesy. Then, if the company sincerely wants you as an artist, it will drop everything and get you your contract.

62

Who to Bother at the Record Company for an Artist Contract

"Bother" is the right word. Even the correct department—A&R—will consider it a nuisance to pop in your cassette, or wind your reel around the heads of an expensive Sony or Teac tapedeck. But A&R is the place to go. A&R, which stands for Artist & Repertoire, is the department in charge of casting the right artists for the label, the right songs for the artist, and the right backup or complementary artists to strengthen the group, if strengthening is needed.

A&R is the equivalent of the editorial department of a book-publishing company. This is where the principal talent-signing decisions are made, rather than in the record production department. Any halfway decent producer will be busy working on new assignments from the label's A&R department. The producer's job is to produce; the A&R person's job is to DECIDE which artists the producer will work with.

Within the A&R department of a major record company, there may be a variety of jobs not related to talent scouting, such as product manager, budget director, and administrative director of A&R. Find out the name of the person who actually listens to demonstration tapes for a living, and send that person your tape. After ten days have gone by, get in touch with this person to find out whether the tape was listened to.

Everyone else—the president of the company, the vice presidents of the company, the heads of marketing, promotion, artist relations, advertising, publicity, and so on—will be too busy with other things to take your demo tape seriously. It is a sign of your professionalism not to bother these people with A&R matters. Many beginners are under the mistaken impression that getting their demo listened to by the top guy in the company is the only way that artists get signed. In fact, the record business is so conservatively run today that a committee decision is practically a precondition for doing anything, especially signing a new artist. The person in charge of the artist acquisition steering committee is the head of A&R, not the president of the company.

A&R people get paid a lot of money to listen to tapes and decide which artists are right for a label. Going above them, in my opinion, is a mistake for unknown artists. If the A&R head doesn't like your demo, it probably means that regardless of whatever other opinions are offered at the company—even those of the owner or president—the label will pass on signing you. If A&R says no, thank them for listening, ask what A&R found objectionable in your music, and go back to the drawing board. You time has not yet come.

63

How to Size Up a Record Company

It follows from our previous discussion of distribution (section 48) that the way to size up a record company has little to do with how many platinum albums adorn the walls of the president's office. In order of importance, artists should ask the following questions:

"What is the record company's distribution capability?"

"What is the record company's marketing capability?"

"How much money will the record company invest to promote each of my records?"

"Who has final control over the product—me or the record company?"

"When will I be paid for my services, and what rights do I have to audit the record company's financial statements relating to my career?"

Let me explain briefly why artists should ask these questions. Distribution, as we all know by now, is the key to financial success. If the record company isn't capable of distributing records internationally and getting paid for those records, the artist may never see a penny of artist royalties.

Without marketing know-how, the distribution arm of the record business (salesmen and record promoters) won't know the best way to sell your product. Very often, the difference between a marginal career and superstardom hinges on marketing insight rather than exceptional musical talent. Artists should definitely meet the record company's marketing mavens before signing a contract. If they've got anything on the ball, they're going to come up with clever ideas after thirty seconds of conversation. The marketing department's overall competency, however, should be gauged by analyzing how many records they've helped place on the Top One Hundred industry trade charts.

If the artist's product is marketed and distributed properly, the money will come—just be patient. Where money is needed initially in the music business is not in the artist's pocket, but in the advertising mix of newspaper and magazine ads, TV and radio commercials, billboards, personal appearances, tour support, publicity, and anything else that will make the artist's product stand out in the marketplace as unique. It may cost more than $1 million in today's business just to take a decent shot at breaking an artist through the almost impenetrable layers of established artists, established consumer attitudes, and multimillion-dollar competing ad campaigns. But that's what the artist wants: a commitment from the record company that they are going to invest a lot of money in developing and promoting the artist's career. Without that money, it will take a miracle for the artist even to become known, let alone become a star or superstar.

Final control is something to discuss prior to signing a contract. The artist and record company should be in agreement on who will decide whether a performance is acceptable; what order the performances will take on the album; how singles are selected for separate release; what the album cover should say and look like; and so on. In order to preserve the business relationship, the artist and record company must be able to get along with each other. In my experience, one of the best ways to insure that business is conducted smoothly is for questions of ultimate authority to be brought out in the open during the contract negotiation.

Finally, though it's not the same as asking for an advance, the artist wants to know when he'll be paid. The artist must also have the right to audit the record company's financial statements relating to the artist's career. While most record companies are run cleanly, some companies are notorious for paying late, or failing to pay 100 percent of what they should, or failing to pay the artist anything. Before signing a record contract, consult with as many informed industry sources as possible.

64

Get a Pocket Calculator, and Use It

Every person in the music business should have a pocket calculator at his side to compute record and publishing royalties. Any calculator with a percentage key will do. A chair is also desirable to help cushion the shock of downside figures, a problem particularly pertinent to beginning artists.

A new recording artist today can anticipate a record royalty on first-released product of 6 percent of the suggested retail list price of an album, which is currently $7.98, less container charges. The container charge, which covers the cost of designing and printing record covers, labels, and sleeves, is the record company's adroit way of knocking off usually 15 percent from the suggested retail list price of an album. This brings the $7.98 figure down to $6.78, according to my calculator, and the artist's royalty from $.478 down to $.406 an album. (Note: Some record companies also pay royalties on 90 rather than 100 percent of records sold. This convention is a carryover from the era of seventy-eight-rpm records, when breakage was a serious factor that supposedly cost the company 10 percent of gross sales. Most major record companies, however, are amenable today to paying artists on 100 percent rather than 90 percent of records sold, PROVIDED the artist asks to be paid on 100 percent during the contract negotiation.)

Ten thousand albums sold, at $.406 an album, equals $4,060. One hundred thousand albums sold, which is an impressive number for an artist's first release, is $40,600. Five hundred thousand albums sold, which entitles the artist to a gold record, is $203,000. One million albums sold, which entitles the artist to a platinum record, is $406,000. It is extremely important, by the way, that records are actually sold to the public and that the record company gets paid for these records by the distributor or dealer. The record business is a consignment business: if product is not ultimately exchanged for cash by consumers, the distributor will return unsold goods to the record company. Artists, unfortunately, do not get paid on returns.

Let us now hypothesize an artist with initial record royalties, on the sale of 100,000 units, of $40,600. The artist has a personal manager who gets 20 percent off the top, which reduces the $40,600 figure to $32,480. The average cost for producing an album today (which is what our hypothetical artist ran up at session costs) is $75,000. This means that the artist owes the record company $34,400. Also, the artist received a $10,000 advance against royalties as a bare subsistence income on which federal, state, and local taxes were paid. This raises the artist's outstanding debt, on his first release, to $44,400.

Now let us suppose that the artist's second album with the record company sells gold: the initial payout, less container charges, is $203,000. The personal manager gets 20 percent, which brings the artist's take down to $162,400. The artist owes $44,400 from the first album, which further reduces the artist's gold record income to $118,000. Finally, the artist spent $100,000 on the second go-round in the studio and took a $15,000 advance. With a gold record on the wall, the artist after two successful album releases still owes the record company $3,000.

Shall we go one step further? On the artist's third try, his record sells platinum. One million albums sold, less 20 percent for the personal manager, nets the artist a royalty of $324,800. The artist owes $3,000 from the second album, plus the artist again spends $100,000 in the studio and takes a $20,000 advance against royalties. This works out to $201,800, which, if the artist isn't prepared, the Internal Revenue Service will substantially swallow up. And on, and on, and on.

Most recording artists, of course, have another ready source of income from live performances, less the 10 to 15 percent commissions to agents and federal, state, and local taxes. If the artist is also a songwriter, his income will certainly be greater than if he is just a performer. But, if we can face the music, our hypothetical artist was also very lucky. Most artists never even approach selling gold, let alone platinum. How do they make a living? How do they survive? It can be very rough for a very long time—perhaps the artist's lifetime. On this sober note, let me recommend the following bits of money-saving advice:

1. *Get as much advance money as you can.*   I said earlier that it is unreasonable for new artists to request six-figure initial advances from record companies. But if you can get $5,000 more from the record company, do it. If the record company wants to advance you $15,000 and you can raise it to $17,500, do it. It may be the only money you ever see from your career as a recording artist.

2. *Keep your production costs down.*   What goes on in most recording studios is sinful. With the proper attitude and an adequately rehearsed ensemble, the cost of produc-

ing many albums could be cut in half. Don't import outside musicians. Don't make long-distance telephone calls from the studio. When you're in the studio, you are there to work. Sit down with the producer and tell him, "I don't want anything fancy. If there's a way to record this selection in two hours instead of six hours, that's what I'd like. I don't want this production to cost a fortune."

3. *Shop around for the best studio deal possible.*   If a studio charges $200 an hour for an album that takes 150 hours to produce, that's $30,000. If another studio in town with the same recording equipment charges $175 an hour for an album that takes 150 hours to produce, that's $26,250, or $3,750 less. Save the money. Learn to think cheap. And much as you might resent it, pick up that pocket calculator and use it every day. If it all comes out of the artist's pocket eventually, the artist has to know the score.

65

Play Power Politics, or Else Feed the Pigeons

Record companies are the most people-intensive entities in the music business. To the outsider they may appear to be stable, professional organizations (some of them actually are), but insiders will tell you that record companies are highly politicized, pressure-cooker environments. Here are some practical tips on getting the most out of the record company and its personnel:

1. *Don't step over people.* Record company employees are extremely sensitive to the cold-shoulder treatment. Artists may want to hobnob exclusively with the president and senior VP's, but it's the lower- and middle-level management cadre, along with their secretaries, who actually do most of the day-to-day work. Snubbing a graphics designer may mean that the artist's record cover is delivered two weeks late. Thumbing one's nose at a product manager's

secretary may result in an important message being "accidentally" thrown away. Every cog in the system is important, and should be treated accordingly.

2. Accept being delegated.   New artists will be assigned to a product manager, record producer, graphics designer, copywriter, and marketing team. Each member of the artist's record company team reports to a superior, who in turn reports to another superior, who in turn reports to senior management. There is a lot of paper work involved in this system, and very little contact between the artist and senior management. But if you want to be a recording artist with a major record company, this is what you're going to be stuck with until you become a superstar. At that time, the record company president may actually return your telephone calls.

3.   Inefficiencies exist at all levels and cannot be changed.   When a scheduled spring release doesn't come out until the fall, when a contract is delivered two weeks after it was supposed to be delivered, when that vital marketing meeting is postponed for the third time due to an illness in the VP's family; then it hits you: the real killer in business is loss of time. There is nothing you can do to change this. If you think it's any better at another company with a large labor force, you're probably mistaken. What you should do is learn to factor inefficiency into the record business equation. If the company says three months, figure it will take six months. If the A&R head says, "I can probably have lunch with you the first week in March," plan to get together around March 15. Next to death, inefficiency is the most unavoidable certainty I know.

4. Be an active, laid-back participant.   Artists who don't stand up for themselves in major companies may literally be lost. But while it is imperative to be actively involved, it is also very important for the artist to know his place. Basically, that place is not the record company proper, but the recording studio. If you want to follow through on an album, which I recommend you do, show respect for the employees whose turf you invade. Be courteous with everyone. Let the record company employees know that you value their professional competencies. Make them feel important; make them feel good about you, too. It is amazing what the right attitude can do to make the system truly excited about launching an artist's career.

5. *Become a favorite.* Within the record company, the artist and personal manager should try to cultivate a senior management sponsor. This person will help steward the artist's career. He may have more weight in more areas of the company than the artist's product manager or record producer. Success in the record business starts with good music, but beyond that politics is essential. If you don't get in there and fight for preferential treatment, you might as well feed pigeons.

66

The Agency Should
Be Your Last Stop

A major agency won't even consider signing an artist today unless the artist already has a recording contract, or is felt to be one agency telephone call away from getting a contract. This makes selecting an agent the last stop in the formation of an artist's management team.

There is another good reason why agents should not be consulted until the artist has already chosen a personal manager, publisher, and record company. If the agent gets to the artist first, the artist may have to pay the agent a 10 percent commission on gross annual income, including record and publishing income. Since booking agents are only peripherally involved with record and publishing companies, it seems unfair for the artist to have to pay an additional 10 percent over and above the personal manager's commission for initiating and negotiating record and publishing deals.

The booking agent's principal domain is the live performance field. This includes concerts, rodeos, carnivals, circuses, and legitimate theatrical showcases. As the artist grows in stature, the agency will also act as the artist's employment adviser and negotiator (in consultation with the artist's personal manager) in related areas, such as motion pictures, radio and TV shows, print ads, commercials, books, and the burgeoning merchandising business (e.g., posters, jewelry, T-shirts).

Competent agents will be recommended by the artist's personal manager and record company. It is important, incidentally, that the three elements—manager, agent, record company—are known to each other and are on amicable terms. In today's business, there is a great need for coordination among these three parties with regard to the artist's business plan, time availability, and willingness to perform.

Artists don't have to say much to prospective agents. The personal manager will do the talking. More to the point, the stature of the artist's record company and personal manager will do the talking. A live showcase may be required prior to signing, but agents generally don't pass on artists who appear destined—by virtue of their first-class affiliations—to be superstars.

If the artist is affiliated with either the American Federation of Musicians or the American Guild of Variety Artists, he can insist that the standard AFM or AGVA agency contract to be used. The term of this contract normally is three years. One-night stands carry an agency commission of 15 percent; engagements of longer duration net the agency the standard 10 percent fee.

Tours will be booked to coincide with the release of an artist's new record product. Any high-powered U.S. agency, such as Premier Talent, ICM, or the William Morris Agency, has the political muscle to distribute talent in the proper talent showcases. Then it's up to the ultimate arbiters of talent—the general public—either to pick up on the artist, or leave the artist to perish.

67

Follow-through Is Essential

It is so tempting to say "Well, I made it. I've got a terrific personal manager, a fantastic music publisher, a superlative record company, and a dynamite booking agent. Now I'm going to set the world on fire."

How do you know this? What guarantees do you have that the record company will even release your first album, or that the publisher will be able to secure a recording by a name artist of your best song? In reality, most newcomers have absolutely nothing that is concrete, bankable, or dependable. Don't be an artist suckered into passivity. Getting into the business isn't the signal to go to sleep; it's the signal to become increasingly vigilant and suspicious of everything that supposedly is being done to help you.

Artists should stay of top of their personal business affairs until they have tangible proof—i.e., a lot of money stashed away—that the business team they've selected can do the job. The operative word here is "follow-through." It can be done either discreetly or overtly, but it is essential that the artist know the bottom line. Above all, artists should hold themselves personally responsible for succeeding or failing in the music business. It's the artist's responsibility to see that the hired help does what it's supposed to do. Various elements may contribute to the artist's demise, but the responsible artist should be able to say, "The fault is ultimately my own, not that of others on my team."

How can artists avoid failure? By working hard. By becoming thick-skinned. By developing a wide-angled view of life. By not abrogating their ultimate responsibility to themselves to succeed. Sure, you need supporting players in the music business, and the best of them do a superlative job. But I think these same successful people would endorse these final words of advice to artists seeking professional careers: never trust anyone completely; follow through on everything you do; and always be on the lookout for Number One—yourself.

PART 6

Record Industry Needs

68

To Become a Record Producer You Must Be Able to Pick Hit Songs

No wonder this is such a coveted career in the music industry. Successful record producers make a ton of money, and are highly esteemed by their peers and the media. Without them, so much of the magic attributed to the artist's genius would never get down on tape. Even though the scramble to become a record producer has gotten much more congested in the last few years, there are still opportunities for ingenious producers with top-notch artists to rise to the top of their profession.

People who want to become producers have much more to prove than their competencies in the studio. What they really must demonstrate to a record company is their ability to pick hit records. Many of the most successful record producers, in fact, began their careers with jobs where they had to listen to a staggering amount of music. Jerry Wexler, for example, was at one time a song plugger for Robbins,

Feist, and Miller. Joel Dorn, who grew up in the same town I did outside Philadelphia, used to be a disc jockey. Jon Landau, who produces Bruce Springsteen, wrote record reviews for *Rolling Stone*. The better you train yourself to hear what actually happens on a record, the better your chances become to develop that indispensable sixth sense for picking hits.

The art of producing hit records involves a combination of creative, administrative, psychological, and business skills honed to a unique personal intensity. The best way to learn how to become a record plugger is to get into the professional studio environment and become a studious observer. This can be accomplished by working at a recording studio in any of several capacities—arranger, audio engineer, assistant audio engineer, floor manager, or general assistant—or by being a member of a group that frequently does sessions in the studio.

Every $125- to $200-an-hour sixteen-track or twenty-four-track studio comes complete with a very capable audio engineer. Many of the most successful record producers know little or nothing about acoustics, audio engineering, or microphone placement. Top producers usually import their favorite audio engineer to handle the board for them while they direct the artist in session. The added expense of an imported audio engineer, of course, is charged to the artist's and the producer's royalty account.

What separates mediocre producers from outstanding producers is the ability of the latter to hear in their minds unique combinations of sound that can be transferred onto magnetic tape. The only way to find out whether you have this ability is to get into the environment, learn what the equipment can do, and begin by recording musicians and vocalists. Anyone can learn the rudiments. Very few, however, have the creative abilities to pick hits, record them properly, and survive the politics of the record business.

69

Find the Right Group, but Keep Your Options Open

Aspiring record producers must have access to up-and-coming, semiprofessional or professional writers, arrangers, and performers. Any legitimate music business job that pays at least a minimal salary and surrounds the aspiring record producer with demo tapes would be fine. Chief among these jobs would be working as a talent scout for a music publisher; working as an assistant in the A&R department of a major label; or working as a talent coordinator of showcase concerts for underground clubs where new artists perform.

Once the right group is found (preferably they will write their own material), the producer will have to take his shot. If the producer is putting up the money to cut a demo, the group should understand that the producer is entitled to at least some financial interest in the master tape if the demo is distributed commercially by a record company. On the other hand, if the aspiring producer is employed in a quasi-production job, he may be invited by his employer to work up a rough demo submitted by the group.

The difference between the two approaches is that the independent producer (i.e., the one who uses his own money) will have a financial stake in the tape, but the music business employee will not have a financial stake—if anything happens with the demo, it all goes to the company that employs him, less the artist's royalty, with perhaps an increase in the producer's salary. Quite a number of aspiring record producers leave the employment of record or music-publishing companies when they think they've stumbled onto a group capable of making hit records.

Once a person leaves a record or publishing company, he may never be able to get his job back. The album may sound great to the aspiring producer, but it may sound horrible to everyone else (I can't say how many times this turns out to be true). I'd like to be able to say, "It never hurts to try," but of course I can't. Still, it is commendable to try—just make sure it doesn't cost every penny of your savings.

70

What to Record:
How Much, How Complete

Consider who you're trying to sell. The head of A&R at a major record company is a harried executive with music coming out of his hair follicles and a snobbish disdain for amateur producers. What you record must sound polished and commercial. The length of the master tape should be short—one song would normally suffice, but go ahead and record two songs for a possible two-sided single release.

The works to record, in this order, are the group's strongest composition and the group's second strongest composition. Never be cute with demos, or use them for the group's experimental music. With a good demo, the producer should be able to deal from strength.

As for the recording studio, by all means shop around for the lowest price you can find. There may be a new studio in town with state-of-the-art equipment, but no clients. Perhaps the group can get by with an eight-track production instead of a sixteen- or twenty-four-track blowout. You may even have a situation where a studio owner offers to eat the production cost in return for a percentage of the master tape. In no case, however, should an aspiring producer spend more than $1,500 of his own money to produce a mixed-down master tape with less than eight minutes of music on it, including dubs.

The right way to think about demo costs is also the most realistic way. They are money down the drain, representing the irrecoverable loss of liquid assets. Live by that reality until you actually get a production deal that gives you an advance-against-royalty check large enough to cover your out-of-pocket production costs.

In all likelihood, you will have to work very hard to get your first deal. Fifty companies may say no; then the fifty-first company may say, "Where have you been? This is just what we've been looking for." In dealing with the fifty companies that said no, remember to be gracious. Remember to ask, "What didn't you like about the tape?" or "Why wasn't the tape right for you?" The best tips on who is presently in the market for your kind of music may come from these casual exchanges.

Never be angry with a turn-down or even a put-down. The door slammed in your face today may be opened wide for you in a year or two, provided you haven't done anything to rule out a potential business arrangement.

71

Don't Get Trapped by the Greed Syndrome

Producing a record for a major record company—nothing more, nothing less—should be the goal of every potential record producer. If you're good, the money will come. If you let greed get in the way of a once-in-a-lifetime opportunity, you are being very foolish. Whatever deal you get initially from a major label, so long as you're the producer and you're getting album credit for being the producer, accept it.

Every so often, about two or three times a year, a producer submits a master tape that's good enough to go straight to the record-pressing and tape-duplicating plant. In a case such as this, the record company may offer to reimburse the producer for his out-of-pocket expenses. Bear in mind, however, that every dollar of production expense is considered an advance against not only the artist's but the producer's record royalties. If the producer can afford to ab-

sorb part of the production cost, he may see production royalties months sooner than a producer who owes substantial
sums to the record company.

If the master demo does its job—i.e., gets the producer a
production deal—but is not considered good enough for
commercial release, the record company may, at its option,
offer to reimburse the producer for it anyway. Then again,
it may not. The demo payback concept is something to discuss in the contract negotiation, but don't count on getting
money back for unusable demos. Failure to recapture this
money, in my opinion, is insufficient cause for walking
away from a potential deal.

Independent record producers may receive production
royalties pegged at 2 percent of the suggested retail list price
of, as an example, a $7.98 album, less 15 percent packaging
allowance ($.135); 3 percent of the suggested retail list
price, less 15 percent packaging allowance ($.20); or 4 per-
cent of the suggested retail list price, less 15 percent packaging allowance ($.27). Obviously, there is a big difference
between getting a 2 percent production royalty and a 4 percent production royalty. It is not always advisable, however, to sign with the company offering the best deal on
paper. When more than one company is vying for a producer's demo (a happy occasion that doesn't happen very
often), the producer should carefully weigh which of the
labels will do the best overall job of selling records, marketing records effectively, and getting the producer his money.

If you want to establish a career as a professional record
producer, you had better stick to your guns and do just that:
produce records. This is not the time to start acting like a
big-shot, wheeler-dealer type production tycoon. Even Jim-
my Guercio, Richard Perry, Kenny Gamble and Leon Huff,
Thom Bell, Charles Koppelman, and Lou Adler had to start
out doing one thing at a time. It should be no different for
you.

The worst thing a record producer can do is to neutralize

his potential stature in the industry by starting out too greedily. If anything, beginners should hold back on their initial financial demands; such discretion will make them appear more attractive to the artists, managers, and record companies without whose business the producer is not in business. Managing acts, publishing their songs, and starting one's own record studio can wait. Get a string of hit records together first—then you can take on the world.

72

Performance Counts: You're Only as Good as Your Last Hit

Producing a finished master is only step two in the hit-making process (step one was signing the producer and artist to a record contract). Step three is packaging and design; step four is the marketing plan; step five is record and tape manufacturing; step six is shipping the product to distributors; step seven is advertising and promotion; step eight is the artist's concert tour and public relations (PR) appearances; step nine is selling the album on the street; step ten is—we hope—getting paid.

Each of the postproduction steps should be looked into by the producer as if the producer's life depended on it (it most certainly may). More talented producers are jobless today not because of what they did in the studio, but because of what they didn't do when their job was supposedly finished. Producers should never trust a record company to do anything the right way. That may sound like a harsh statement, but until a record company proves different from the norm, the producer should check into every phase of the business and see to it that things go according to schedule.

Otherwise, the way you got to be a record producer is also the way you get to stay being a record producer. You're only as good as your last hit. Whatever it takes for you to stay on top of changing tastes in music, changing methods of record production, changes in record company personnel, and changes in your own personal life, you're going to have to do it. The responsibility for this rests squarely on your own shoulders (see section 67).

If you start out with a string of hits, you're bound eventually to get a lot of attractive financial offers from different record companies. Always remember, though, how it started. Someone in the A&R department said to you, "I think you've got good ears. I think you've picked a hit song for us, and maybe a hit artist to sing it." As soon as the money means more to you than the quality of the artist's music, your days as a desired hit record producer will be numbered. If the song doesn't have it—if the artist can't possibly be a star—no matter how enticing the deal appears to be, my advice is to tell the artist's sponsor, "Sorry, but I pass."

73

How to Start
an Independent
Record Company

Years before the advent of double-digit inflation, men like
Ahmet Ertegun, Jerry Moss and Herb Alpert, Neil Bogart,
Bob Reno, and Henry Stone started their respective record
companies (Atlantic Records, A&M Records, Casablanca
Records, Midland International Records, and TK Records)
on shoestring budgets. The cost of that shoestring budget today has risen to hundreds and hundreds of thousands of
dollars a year, making the idea of starting an independent
record company the most irrational, pie-in-the-sky scheme
for the complete beginner.

I shall deal with this subject perfunctorily because many
readers no doubt are curious to learn how it's done. But
unless you have years of front-line record experience and access to very wealthy investors, you should not under any circumstances give serious thought to forming your own
independent label in the '80s.

The fundamental ingredient in launching a successful independent record company is either a great artist or a unique recording concept. These are the hooks for attracting a syndicate of music business pros with good ears, who will consider it a prudent gamble to buy stock in a new record company if they hear something really extraordinary in the artist, and in the person seeking funding.

Banks will laugh you out of their offices if the purpose for requesting a $500,000 loan is to start an independent record company. Believe it or not, one of the best places to look for money is overseas. Some of the major European music and publishing companies may be willing to advance sizable sums if, in return, they receive favorable long-term licensing deals from the U.S.-based operation. An ideal place to meet wheeler-dealer European music business magnates is the annual MIDEM convention held in Cannes. So long as one monster hit emerges from the record company's first album, the foreign backer's return-on-investment yield may prove to be excellent.

People who start independent record companies must plan to handle every step in the record operation themselves, except retail sales—that job would be handled by the independent record company's distributor, either a major label like CBS, Warner, or RCA, or a combination of independent record distributors around the country. This is why such outlandish sums of money are needed to capitalize the business. Five hundred thousand dollars must pay the executive salaries of an operations director, national promotion director, director of publishing, product manager, and office staff, plus office overhead, plus the president's salary (see section 27), plus record and tape manufacturing costs, plus jacket fabrication costs, and so on, ad infinitum.

Five hundred thousand dollars will go down the tubes in flash, and what will you have to show for it, other than an ulcer? You hope at least one piece of superior product, and a superior marketing plan to back it up. But what a gamble.

What a terrible price to pay if the record company owner loses (Hint: Most investors will not take a $500,000 loss sitting down). This is why more and more independent record companies are getting out of the independent record business and going into the custom label business, which is covered in the next section.

74

The Custom Label Compromise

A custom label may be a glorified independent production deal giving the producer his own label identification (e.g., Planet Records, Richard Perry's recently formed custom label, is distributed by Elektra/Asylum Records, which in turn is distributed by Warner/Elektra/Atlantic). A custom label may, in fact, be an independent record company, such as Midland International Records was during the period that it was distributed by RCA. What every custom label deal has in common is that the distributing label pays for the production, manufacturing, and promotion of the custom label's product. In return for taking this added financial risk, the distributing label does not purchase records from the custom label; instead, it pays the custom label a royalty on every record or tape sold for which the distributor has received payment.

The highest custom label record royalty today is 20 percent of the suggested retail list price of an album, less container charges. For a $7.98 album, this means that the custom label owner will receive $1.35 per record sold from the distributor. How much of this custom label royalty is subsequently paid to the artists and record producers signed to the custom label is between the custom label owner and his artist-producer employees.

The nice thing about custom label deals is that they provide enough advance money for the custom label owner to continue being independent. The major problem with custom label deals is the custom label owner's loss of control over his product. The custom label owner may continue to own the master tapes, but the manufacturing of records and tapes is handled by the distributing label. Promotion, publicity, and sales are also normally controlled by the distributor, which for better or for worse (usually worse, according to my sources) places the custom label totally at the mercy of the distributing label.

A really strong custom label owner will be able to sit down with a potential distributor and say, "Let's not kid ourselves. When push comes to shove, your company will take care of its own line of records first. So I want more control over my product. I want you to advance me enough money so that I can hire my own national promotion director and my own product manager. I don't want to have to rely on your own people to do the job." This, I think, is an excellent argument.

I have only one more thing to say about starting a custom label. A custom label deal must be earned. Beginning record producers should not even mention the words "custom label" to a record company. First they should produce a hit record, then another hit record, then another hit record, and then still another hit record. The difference in responsibility between being an independent record producer and being a custom label owner is huge. If you're not cut out to be a business finder, office manager, and contract negotiator, the custom label business is not for you.

75

Get the Best People
You Can for the Jobs
in Your Company

There was a story recently about a $15 million dollar rip-off of U.S. taxpayer's money that involved the unauthorized use of Government Service Bureau gasoline credit cards. That's what can happen when the federal government dangles fringe benefits in front of the wrong type of government employee. That's what happens every day, too, though on a somewhat smaller scale, in the record business. Employees steal money under the cover of their expense accounts. Other employees may be using their jobs as a front for pushing drugs. The best way to prevent this from happening is to have eyes like a hawk, not be afraid to question an employee, and to fire anyone who abuses your trust.

Next to pure desire, the most important success ingredient in business is choosing the right employees. It certainly accounts for why some record companies do far better financially than other record companies. Unfortunately, there is no tried and true method for choosing the right people. It is a talent, however, that can be cultivated.

In business, the employees you want should be seasoned individuals, ready and eager to work for their salary. Don't hire friends. Keep your lover out of the office. Interview a lot of different people for an important job, and make it a point not only to get referrals, but to pick up the telephone and ask a previous employer, "What did you think of this employee?"

Just because a person has worked in the record business for five years doesn't mean he's the best person for the job. A shoe salesman, with the proper motivation and a little training, might turn into a superior record promoter. An insurance broker may have transferrable skills for becoming a fantastic product manager. Intelligence, honesty, motivation, character: these are the primary things to look for. Brand-name affiliations, in my opinion, are secondary.

76

Getting Paid
Is a Two-sided Affair

Since by now we have introduced both sides of the record-manufacturing business—the production component, which is either the custom label, staff producer, or an independent record producer, and the distributing component, which is either a major U.S. label with its own national distribution network or the independent record distributors—I see no reason why, for the sake of brevity, we can't look at the sensitive issue of payment as a two-sided affair.

Streetwise record producers understand the true meaning of the industry phrase, "You're only as good as your last hit." If the producer is hot, he will be paid promptly. If the producer is lukewarm, he will be paid, but the distributor—citing slow returns from his dealers—will stall payments, or offer to pay the producer a token amount of his projected royalties in that accounting period.

If the producer is cold, he may never get paid. A distrib-

utor may size up a struggling production company and conclude, "They're not going to sue us if we don't pay them
because they don't have any money to sue us." Needless to
say, one of the cardinal rules that beginning producers
should learn is to spread their hits out over a long period of
time. When the hits stop, the money may stop, too.

Generally speaking, distributors like to hold onto money
as long as they can. Producers, on the other hand, like to get
paid advances and royalties as soon as possible. The principal devices used by distributors to stall payments to the
producer are the semiannual accounting period and the
concept of reserves, or returns. Producers will not be able to
negotiate changes in either of these conventions. What they
should know up front, however, is the basis upon which returns are computed. Since the record business is truly international, and since reports of returns from U.S. dealers and
foreign licensees may be slow in getting back to the
distributor's head office, it is strongly recommended that
producers try to negotiate a very long auditing period—
three years or more—for each of the semiannual accounting
periods during which they are in business with the distributor.

Pirated or counterfeit records, which are manufactured
and sold without payment to the record's copyright owner,
injure producers and distributors equally. (Note: This alleged $200-million-a-year industry was dealt a severe blow
in December 1978 when 300 FBI agents impounded $100
million worth of modern sound-recording equipment in
nineteen separate raids. Officials are claiming to have
"wiped out 50 percent" of U.S. piracy operations, according
to the *New York Times*,) Otherwise, most deals provide that
the record producer's royalties on tape product be half the
basic production royalty for first-release album product.
Records sold outside the United States usually net the producer one-half his basic royalty, as well. The producer receives nothing on promotional records, cut-outs, and prod-

uct sold at salvage value. Budget record royalties are a fraction of the basic production royalty; so, too, are royalties derived from TV direct-mail advertising promotions. Normally, records sold through record clubs yield the producer 50 percent of his basic royalty.

These are standard industry royalty rates that apply to artists as well as producers. They are subject to change once the producer has demonstrated the ability to supply hit records. Whether they are right or wrong, good or bad, is really not the issue (see section 33). The producer and distributor should both be very careful with money. Theirs is a business relationship before anything else, and as we should all know by now, looking out for Number One is what business, basically speaking, is about.

77

Tips on the Retail Record Business

Record retailers sell discs, tapes, cartridges, cassettes, sheet music, and accessories to walk-in customers. Depending on the size of their pocketbooks, a record retailer should begin either with a specialty store concentrating in classical, country, jazz, international, or oldies records, or a full-line store offering catalog selection (i.e., everything a particular artist has recorded) along with a complete line of records in all price and content categories.

The three most important factors affecting survival in the retail record business are price, location, and proper merchandising of the store. No retail establishment is big enough yet to control competition; consequently, retailers cannot influence the price at which they sell product. Where price does become a significant factor is at the other end of the business. A large retailer who also acts as a subdistributor (one-stop) will be able to buy product from manufacturers at what is called the wholesale-wholesale price, rather than the wholesale-retail price (in some circles this is referred to as the "schmuck price") reserved for retail-only type establishments. The wholesale-wholesale price on a $7.98 LP currently fluctuates between $3.75 and $4.03; the wholesale-retail price, by comparison, is a flat $4.20. Subdistributors may also receive favorable price reductions unavailable to retail-only establishments on product exported outside the United States.

The importance of location ties into the modus operandi of the retail record business. Records are often sold on a barter basis. If the retailer is situated in a high-traffic location, a record salesman may offer to give the retailer bonus records (freebies) or added discounts in exchange for window space, in-store airplay, and the use of customer mailing lists. (Note: Artists and producers receive no royalties on product offered as free goods.)

The proper way to negotiate seller-buyer deals is to wait for the salesman to approach the retailer with an offer. Deals involving added discounts range from 10 to 50 percent off the regular wholesale price. In cases where the record company is trying to get in-store exposure for a new or comeback artist, the deal may be one-for-one, as in "Buy one record, get one free." Obviously, retailers with prime locations have a much better chance to profit from these barter arrangements than do hole-in-the-wall operations.

The other critical survival factor—merchandising the store properly—should be addressed after the retailer has decided whether to start a full-line or specialty store. Merchandising, in this case, means that the retailer must have enough inventory on hand so that there is product in the store to sell. Most manufacturers award retailers a 2 percent discount if the retailer pays his bills on time. Inside the store, the biggest problems retailers have are customer shoplifting and—sad to say—employee shoplifting.

People interested in careers in the retail record business or the independent record distribution business, which is analogous, should apprentice first with an established firm and see if they like the work. Record companies generally shy away from investing in retail establishments, but private investors and commercial banks are available to help finance a carefully planned retail venture. They are impressed with the fact, as I am, that since the end of World War II the general public's appetite for buying records and tapes has continued to skyrocket.

78

Getting a Job with a Record Company

Basically there are three ways to get a job in the business today. The first way, the so-called jugular approach, is to contact someone you know on the inside and ask for a job.

The second way is to become a college rep. A rep is a full-time college student who helps get airplay for new releases on the campus radio station. College reps may also be involved in selling records to the campus record store, and in helping to coordinate local appearances by the company's touring artists. After graduation, the cream of the college reps are invited to join the record company as low-level managers. If you're still in high school and would like to become a college rep, get on the telephone with major record companies, find out whether they have a college rep program, and ask for particulars on how to apply.

The third way to get a job in the business is to become an acknowledged leader in a music business–related profession.

Chief among these professions, in my experience, are record retailing, radio, television, law, accounting, and investment analysis. Quite a few record companies, it seems, prefer hiring managers from outside the profession. On the one hand, getting new blood into the business helps things from going stale. On the other hand, it is ironic that one of the recommended ways for getting a job with a record company is to veer off on a tangent. That, however, is how some people in the business today got their jobs.

I don't subscribe to any of the textbook ways for getting a job in the record industry. Waiting on line at the personnel office is a waste of time. Sending letters is a waste of time and postage stamps. Even if you're black, hispanic, female, or a member of some other minority group, you can't expect your minority standing to exert any significant influence over a record company's hiring practices. Who you know makes all the difference (see sections 1 and 5).

Seeking employment in the record business is an excellent opportunity to assess one's ability and dedication to succeed. It is not supposed to be easy to get a job. It will require you to be resourceful. It will require you to make hundreds of phone calls. It will require you to struggle for months, if not years. But if you really want it, you're going to make it one day. That's what you have to keep thinking. Above any other consideration, the key to getting a job in the music business is never, *never* to give up.

PART 7

Music Publishing Needs

79

Publishing Is the Best Business to Be In

If you're not sure which music business to get into, try music publishing first. It doesn't take a lot of money to start a publishing company, and it is a high income-generating business. The publisher's copyrights are tangible assets that can perhaps be used as collateral for bank loans or substantial cash investments. It's a high-energy, international business with direct links to every other conceivable music industry. Most important, it gives the successful publisher lifetime income, plus another fifty years of income for the publisher's estate. Publishing represents the only guaranteed form of multi-year security available to music industry professionals.

The basis for this economic bounty is the U.S. copyright law, a copy of which may be obtained at no charge—along with a comprehensive booklet called "General Guide to the Copyright Act of 1976"—by writing the Copyright Office,

Library of Congress, Washington, D.C. 20559. The purpose of copyright is to insure that authors and publishers of works will have a financial interest in their works. The principal method of securing this right is the concept known as permissions (see section 45). Once copyright has been properly secured, the publisher is entitled to income for the following uses:

Recording.   Every time a record or tape of a publisher's song is sold to the public, the publisher receives what is called a mechanical royalty from the record company. Under the 1909 copyright law, the mechanical royalty was fixed at $.02 per song. With the passage of the 1976 copyright law, however, mechanical royalties have risen to either $.0275 per song or $.005 for every minute of recorded music, whichever is greater.

Performance.   Every time a copyrighted piece of music is broadcast on the radio or TV, the publisher gets paid. Any works performed publicly for profit in a concert hall, theater, nightclub, skating rink, carnival, or discotheque generate publishing income. Background music in elevators, restaurants, hotel lobbies, aircraft, and other business establishments net the publisher still more money. The means by which these moneys are collected are blanket performing rights licenses. These earnings are the single largest source of worldwide publishing income.

Synchronization.   Music heard on the soundtrack of a motion picture, commercial, or TV film pays the publisher a negotiated fee. Major motion pictures pay more than educational TV shorts, but every commerical user must pay the publisher something.

Grand, or theatrical.   Music that is featured in a theatrical show is also income generating for the music publisher. Fees are negotiated directly between the publisher and the theatrical producer.

Foriegn. United States publishers license foreign publishers to promote their copyrights in exchange for a share in international publishing royalties. Depending on how strong the U.S. publisher's copyrights are, the U.S Publisher's percentage of foreign publishing income may run anywhere from 15 to 95 percent, less direct business-related expenses.

Print. Music publishers have for hundreds of years made money by selling printed sheet music—piano-vocal copies, arrangements, and folios—to amateur and professional musicians.

Merchandising. Publishers have just begun to capitalize on the licensing of famous first pages or lines of music to T-shirt manufacturers and poster companies.

Many service organizations exist to help the publisher collect money in each of there areas. ASCAP, BMI, and SESAC specialize in licensing and collecting performing rights. The Harry Fox Agency, the American Mechanical Rights Association (AMRA), and the Walter Hofer Organization specialize in negotiating mechanical and synchronization rights. Any number of outstanding music business lawyers may be able to negotiate better foreign, print, and grand rights deals for the publisher than can the publisher himself. But this is not the real key to becoming a successful publisher. The real key to making it as a publisher has been, and will continue to be, the rare ability to pick future hit songs.

80

Sell the Songwriter on Your Personal Merits

Why should an unpublished songwriter with hit potential written all over his songs bother to sign with a new publisher? If I were the publisher, I'd argue my case as follows:

A publisher's job is to get business for a songwriter. A songwriter's job is to turn out hit song after hit song after hit song. The songwriter's interests would be better served in the long run by having me handle the business while the songwriter continues to concentrate on songs.

The fact that I'm a new publisher means that I am very hungry. My personal survival hinges on getting business for the songwriter. I can't afford to jeopardize my reputation by giving the songwriter a bad deal. The songwriter will get faster service, personal attention, and fair treatment from start to finish with me.

I'm not a novice in this business. I know the heads of A&R at all the major record companies. I am on a first-name basis with more than a dozen major record producers.

When I telephone a VIP personal manager, agent, or music business lawyer, my phone calls are taken. I am not intimidated by superstars, and am on speaking terms with more than one. If who you know is nine-tenths of success in the music business (and it is), I would seem to have that base covered pretty well.

I understand how the publishing business works. The principal cast of characters at ASCAP, BMI, SESAC, AMRA, NMPA (National Music Publishers Association), and the Harry Fox Agency are known to me. I am aware that ASCAP might be better for a particular songwriter than BMI, or vice versa. I am familiar with some of the tricks of the trade that, when applied, may double or triple a songwriter's earnings from a single release. Personal experience would definitely be one of my strongest attributes for selling the songwriter.

I will offer the songwriter a good deal. I wouldn't sign an AGAC contract (see section 60), but I will give the songwriter his copyright back after two years. I will exert my best efforts at all times, and my field of interest will be limited exclusively to music publishing. The songwriter and I will be fifty-fifty partners on everything except print rights—there, depending on how many copies are sold, I'll pay the songwriter between $.06 and $.10 for each piano-vocal copy, and between 10 and 17.5 percent of the retail price of a folio. The songwriter will get semiannual royalty statements from me, and the songwriter will have an open-ended right to inspect, during normal working hours, my financial records relating to the songwriter's career.

That would be my basic argument. As a matter of fact, it would seem that on paper I do have impressive credentials for becoming a music publisher. (Note: For what it's worth, if I truly had the interest in becoming a music publisher, I probably wouldn't be writing this book. Such are the reasons why some people drive Rolls-Royce convertibles, and others Volkswagen Beetles.)

The purpose of this exercise, however, was to make the reader aware of the devices normally used by professional publishers to influence songwriters to sign. If you have contacts, experience, and a complete understanding of music-publishing practices, you might go ahead and set up your own publishing company. But if you are deficient in just one of these areas, you should not expect an intelligent songwriter to consider you as a serious contender for his publishing business.

81

Don't Incorporate: A Sole Proprietorship Will Do the Job

There is no need for a newcomer to music publishing to spend hundreds of dollars on incorporation. A sole proprietorship or partnership will do fine. All that is necessary to become a sole proprietor is to go to a stationery store, pick up a DBA (Doing Business As) blank form, fill out the form, have it notarized, and file it with the office in charge of new business at town or city hall. The cost of becoming a sole proprietor, not including transportation to and from the stationery store and city hall, should be under $15.

The safest name to use for a publishing company is the individual's full name or initials, such as "John Doe Music" or "J.D. Publishing." People who think up more original names may get into difficulty if the name they've chosen is already registered as a trademark or service mark (see section 45). When you're starting up, the safest, least expensive way to go is eminently preferable.

The publishing firm should be a one-person operation at the beginning. Don't even hire a secretary until your songs have begun to be charted consistently. If you need multiple copies of demos, look around for the cheapest duplicating center. You might be better off buying a fairly decent tape recorder and playback deck and making your own demos. Business should be conducted out of the beginning publisher's home, never at an office.

People don't stand on ceremony in the music business. You can be the most unpleasant person in creation, but if you have the ability to pick hit songs, your place in the music business will be secure.

82

Select the Right
Publishing Team

Publishers, at their option, may elect either to handle all their business dealings themselves, or to farm work out to specialized agencies. Here are some tips on choosing an appropriate course of action for your firm.

1. Performing rights.   Not even the specialists—ASCAP, BMI, and SESAC—know precisely how many performances a musical composition receives in a year. Each society, however, has an effectively proven worldwide system for surveying performances and collecting license fees. Membership in the societies is available and practically free to all publishers. The question, then, is not whether the publisher should develop his own performing rights licensing system; the question is, with which of the three performing-rights societies should the publisher affiliate?

Since ASCAP, BMI, and SESAC are essentially in the

same business (of the three, only SESAC is also involved in licensing mechanical and synchronization fees), they must be very competitive in wooing the brightest publishing prospects into their respective folds. Each society today will be prepared to offer an advance against royalties. Beyond that, ASCAP's strongest selling points are its superior logging system and aggressive history of suing delinquent users. BMI, which started twenty-six years later than ASCAP and is still trying to catch up, offers a unique bonus plan that doubles the publisher's earnings beyond designated performance parameters. BMI is also the most liberal society with advance money.

SESAC, the smallest of the three societies, is particularly strong in country music, and has an excellent reputation for personal service and prompt payment. Shop around, by all means. Ask about advances, bonuses, what the society can do to get more business for the publisher, and under what conditions the publisher can leave the society, if the publisher so chooses.

2. Mechanical rights.   If the publisher's works are coverable—i.e., other vocalists and instrumentalists will want to record the work after the initial record release— there is a more persuasive argument for involving an outside agent. Also, if there are hundreds or thousands of copyrights to look after, it might be better to go outside. The other key consideration is the publisher's experience quotient. Not every song is actually sold to a record company for $.0275. If a major recording artist decides to do the publisher a big favor and record his song, contingent on receiving 50 percent of the publisher's mechanical income from that song, the publisher who licenses his own mechanicals has to know how to field such a request (a consensus of veteran publishers would accept the offer with gratitude).

Still, some publishers don't need a Harry Fox–type agency. Harry Fox, for example, charges the publisher between

4.25 and 5 percent of the publisher's annual mechanical income under $25,000, and between 3.25 and 3.5 percent of the publisher's annual mechanical income over $25,000. A small firm with a limited number of noncoverable songs might do better saving the money, provided the publisher has experience negotiating mechanical license fees.

3. Synchronization, grand, and international rights.   The twin tests here are experience and time. Experienced publishers relish getting telephone inquiries from potential users. They can go one-on-one with anybody, and they have much more knowledge about the content of their works than the agent. But time is of the essence in the publishing business. If the publisher is involved primarily with creative work—i.e., coaching songwriters, producing demos, or selling concepts to artists and producers—the involvement of a competent agent may be essential.

Again, it is advisable to shop around for the best deal possible. Some lawyers will do this work on a time basis; others will insist on getting a percentage of the publisher's synchronization, grand, and international rights annual income. Because of inflation, the Harry Fox Agency, SESAC, AMRA, and the Walter Hofer Organization will probably raise their publisher-related service fees in the near future. A quick series of telephone calls should answer the vital question of how much the agent's commission will be.

4. Print rights.   It's almost impossible today for an unattached publisher's sheet music to be exposed properly in retail stores. Most sheet music is sold in racks. Since there are a limited number of racks in every store, the print music distributor has to present his customers with the strongest possible merchandise. Invariably, these are deluxe folios featuring the music of Joan Baez, Paul Simon, Bob Dylan, songs recorded by Elvis Presley, John Denver, and the Beatles, along with the hottest new singer-songwriter phenomenons.

I'm a big advocate of taking the initiative in most cases, but on the subject of print music I'd counsel people to wait for somebody else to take the initiative. Wait for a full-service manufacturer and distributor, such as Warner Brothers Music, to say, "We've been watching the progress of your songwriter on the charts. Now we'd like to make you an offer on print music." Doing it the reverse way, frankly, is a waste of time.

As always, the publisher should keep close tabs on how well his music-publishing team is actually performing. It would be highly advantageous if the publisher, as a condition for staying signed to a particular team member, can negotiate a schedule of guaranteed payments (from the team member to the publisher) based on attainable objectives. Short of this, the key concept to establish between the parties is that they are venturing forth on a trial basis only.

83

Never Stop Thinking about Publishing

Music publishing used to be a two-penny business. Today, because of the 1976 U.S. copyright law, it's a two and three-quarter penny business. Sooner or later, every successful publisher decided to cash in on his industry connections and become a record producer, custom label owner, or personal manager. Notwithstanding exceptions to the rule, such as Paul Simon, John Lennon, and Paul McCartney, whose annual publishing incomes are in the millions of dollars, multiplatinum album publishers-turned-producers can expect to realize seven- or eight-figure annual incomes. Publishing, on the other hand, may generate only (only!) a six-figure annual income.

But consider this. Long after the Internal Revenue Service has siphoned off most of the seven- or eight-figure annual income, long after the multiplatinum album's selling life is over—for fifty years, in fact, after the author of the

239

composition has departed this planet—a hit song can be making money for whoever has an interest in that song's copyright. This reality makes music publishing, over the course of a person's lifetime, far more lucrative and much more desirable a profession than owning a record label, producing records, or managing artists. In summary, while it may be expedient to diversify into other areas of the music business, if you're lucky enough to write hit songs or to get a piece of a hit song's publishing income, you would be insane to turn your back on music publishing completely.

Hit songwriting ability is the music business talent I most envy. Learning how to pick hit songs may take years, just as songwriting can't be learned overnight, but if there are any skills worth studying, I'd have to put those two—songwriting and publishing—at the top of the list. Then, if you're talented, make sure you hold onto your copyrights. Don't sell them cheaply; better yet, don't sell them at all. Thanks to the U.S. copyright law, a copyright to a hit song is the closest thing to solid gold.

PART 8

Management and Agency Needs

84

What It Really Means to Be a Manager or Agent

Let's start with the dissimilarities between managers and agents. Personal managers are always on the road with their artists; agents are tied to the telephone and stay close to home or office.

Personal managers can only handle one or two artists at the beginning; on the other hand, agents may get into business with a dozen or more artists.

Managers must be totally involved with everything their artists are planning to do, now and in the future, both professionally and in their personal lives; agents, whose interests are more highly focused, are primarily concerned with getting employment for the artist—specifically concert engagements—in the immediate future.

Managers must have excellent musical taste and the ability to pick hits; agents needn't know anything about music— they tend to let the artist's record company affiliation, album sales, and general notoriety do the choosing of their artist roster for them.

A successful personal manager will have a small office and a small office staff; a successful agent will have at least one large office and dozens, if not hundreds, of employees.

Managers, whose profession outside the state of California is basically unregulated, may enter business with no restrictions and move about as they wish; agents, whose profession is watched carefully by the entertainment unions and departments of state government, may have to be bonded by the state and obtain franchise certificates from the various entertainment unions as a prerequisite for opening a business.

Managers may have to make substantial financial investments in order to develop the artist's career properly; agents, whose overhead costs are far greater, normally do not advance money to artists.

Managers make anywhere from 20 to 50 percent of the artist's gross annual income; agents charge lower commissions, between 10 and 15 percent but make up the difference by doing a large volume of business.

Now for the similarities. These are both unglamorous professions. Talented managers and agents tend to overlap in their cerebral contributions to the packaging and merchandising of artists. Neither the manager nor the agent can expect to become rich overnight. The competition in both fields is tremendous, and it's getting tougher all the time. Both businesses require a very tight rein over the artist, primarily to prevent the artist from doing what so many struggling artists, tired of waiting, are tempted to do: dump their present manager or agent for a supposed better deal.

These are highly speculative businesses. For every manager or agent who makes it, there are hundreds of financially ruined failures. Managers and agents must be high-stakes gamblers willing to take a chance not only with money but with irreplaceable years from their lives. Both professions require a high toleration for getting along with other people and accepting human error.

Management and agency work requires a tremendous amount of concentrated effort at the beginning. The work can't be done haphazardly; it has to be eighteen-hour-a-day, highly focused work. If you want to emerge as a successful manager or agent, you can't afford to give it less than your total undivided attention. Then, as always, success is a combination of being in the right place at the right time, luck, and dedication.

Neither of these businesses is for dispassionate people, which underscores the most peculiar element common to management and agency work: the unbusinesslike manner in which business is conducted. If you are ordered, reasonable person, you probably don't belong in either of these professions. If, on the other hand, you are a somewhat crazed visionary (I mean this as a compliment) with the ability to think creatively and objectively (about money) at the same time, either of these professions offers dynamic opportunities for an exciting career.

85

Start the Business with a Known-entity Artist

All new artists are not alike. Some of them may have access to money. Others may have important industry connections, but no track record. A few will have impressive singer-songwriting abilities, but neither money or stature. None of these potential artists, in my opinion, should be considered as candidates for the very important role of first artist signed to a manager or agent.

The fastest way to get somewhere in the management-agency business is to pin one's hopes on a known entity. The ideal artist has a good track record with clubs, concert promoters, record companies, radio and TV talk show hosts, and the print media. Preferably, the artist is a person rather than a group, a fresh face with a new story to tell rather than a comeback artist. Such an artist, with the proper sales pitch, will be seen as a seasoned professional on the threshold of a successful career in the legitimate music business.

It really doesn't matter where the artist comes from, so long as the manager or agent can produce charts, newspaper clippings, and perhaps TV footage attesting to the artist's abilities and popularity. The artists best fitting this description may not be U.S. artists, but of international origin. These artists, whether they reside in the United Kingdom, France, Holland, Australia, or elsewhere, may be able to make big dollars for a manager or agent in a relatively short period of time.

If the international artist already has a foreign manager, the U.S. manager or agent should try to negotiate a submanager or subagency deal with the United States, Canada, and Mexico included in the territory (there's nothing wrong with trying for the entire northern hemisphere, either). The submanager or subagent's argument is as follows: he is a resident American, fluent in English, with a vast knowledge of American tastes in music and other forms of entertainment; he can advise the international manager how best to package the artist for the U.S. market; he can promote the international artist's product speedily and efficiently, using his American music industry contacts in concert with the international manager's U.S. connections; he will be Johnny-on-the-spot for the international manager in the event that direct intervention is needed when the international manager is unavailable to provide it; he will take direction from the international manager and sign a pledge that he will not steal the artist; and he will work for a negotiable percentage (between 10 and 50 percent) of the artist's gross annual income derived from the U.S. submanager's or subagent's territory.

Even if the U.S. manager or agent can't sign the international artist directly, the exposure gained from working with a major artist may prove to be invaluable. Once an unknown manager or agent gains access to the legitimate music business and its cadre of VIP executives, his battle for survival may essentially be over. If the manager or agent is considered a first-rate pro, he will soon receive enticing offers to represent other promising artists, not as a subagent but as a full-fledged management equal.

The other way to secure a known-entity artist is to become friendly with an established artist who is unhappy with his present manager or agent. Such artists have a tendency to break away from their manager or agent, start their own management company, and offer employment opportunities to their friends. If, however, this is not the artist's intention, the enterprising manager or agent might offer to buy the artist's contract from the present manager or agent. Such requests are commonplace in the music business, and would account for the inclusion in virtually every entertainment contract of an assignment clause.

86

First Get a Job with an Established Manager or Agent

Working in the mail room of the William Morris Agency has, for many years, epitomized what is good and practical about getting an apprenticeship in the music business. From low-level jobs such as these, talented newcomers have assimilated knowledge, impressed company management, and risen occasionally to spectacular heights within the industry. Here are some tips on how to get a job with a management or agency firm:

1. Stay in touch. Owing to general employee dissatisfaction with niggardly salaries and nonmanagerial work, there is a rapid labor turnover at most firms. If at first you don't succeed, make a repeat visit about a week later, and a week after that, and a week after that. I remember, by illustration, one guest instructor at the Zadoc Institute who spotted a one-time job applicant with his company in class. "What happened to you?" the guest instructor asked. "I got discouraged after ten tries, you know, so I gave up," the student replied. "Gee, that's too bad," the guest instructor said. "I was just getting to know your face, and I was planning to offer you a job the next time I saw you."

2. Offer to work for very low wages. Getting into the management or agency firm to learn what you can and show what you can do is the primary objective. Making a decent wage should be a tertiary consideration for beginners.

3. Be careful what you say. Employers, as a rule, do not like to hire potential competitors. They are interested in hiring capable young people at low wages who will be satisfied working in a specialized area (so that they can't learn the entire business), and who will take direction from the employer without protest. Some people are more equipped than others to shield their long-term career aspirations, but in either case—whether or not you intend to open your own firm one day—the words you say and the manner in which you say them will make or break your chance for a job. Be low-keyed; be sincere; be intelligent, but not overpowering in your brilliance.

4. Do a good job. It may not matter whether you're fired, promoted, or unable to continue work. Once you're in, you're bound to be exposed to other people. It is amazing how few secrets there are in the music business with regard to the competencies and personalities of the labor force. If you have an untarnished reputation and at least one established, reputable music business pro willing to act as a referral, you have what it takes to get ahead, regardless of whether there was a falling out between you and your original employer.

87

Six More Success Tips

The following suggestions are intended to help beginning managers and agents avoid disaster:

1. Break one artist at a time.   The music business doesn't award points to the agent with the largest roster of artists, or the manager with the most diversified interests. Every ounce of the manager's and agent's initiative should be channeled initially into their keystone artist. Every drop of the manager's and agent's creative juices should fuel the breaking of that artist, and that one artist alone. Once the artist has established a good reputation for the manager and agent, the rest becomes easy.

2. Make a capital investment in the artist.   The most expedient way to retain the artist's services is to see to it that the artist owes money to the manager. The more money the artist owes, the less likely the artist is to breach the management agreement. (Note: I am assuming here that the manager has not selected a weirdo act; whatever the act does onstage is fine, but they had better be reasonable human beings offstage who understand what can happen if they're sued). Investing in his own acts—i.e., putting money back into the business—also helps reduce the manager's business profits and personal income, which, in turn, adjusts the manager's tax obligations in the salutary, downward direction. The only way an act should be able to leave a manager is with the manager's permission, or if another organization offers to buy the artist's contract from the manager.

3. Be a friend and counselor to the artist.   In order for the act to be broken, it may be necessary to run the 200-concerts-a-year gauntlet. That is a lot of energy, sore throats, and frazzled nerves going out, and it has to be replenished. The artist, the manager, and the agent must truly care for each other as human beings. They must give as well as they take. The product isn't records or copyrights, but a sensitive group of human beings. Whatever it takes for the artist to feel confident, enthusiastic, and eager to play for his audience, the manager and agent must provide it.

4. Try to get paid in cash.   When a buyer, such as a club or theater, stops payment on a check, or the check bounces, the manager and agent lose credibility with the artist. More to the point, the manager and agent lose the income from that concert. The operative condition for undertaking business as a manager or agent is total distrust of anything that moves. If a club wants your act, they have to pay cash before the act walks out onstage. Fifty percent of the talent fee should be paid in advance by certified check. In order to maintain the artist-manager-agent mutual admiration society, it is essential to receive guaranteed payment, never personal or business checks.

5. Get power of attorney from the artist.   Management and agency work requires rapid decisions, the ability to get into or out of deals quickly, and latitude to direct the artist's career along prescribed guidelines. Artists should not be back-seat drivers with their manager and agent. Artists should keep abreast of what is happening (see section 67), but they should also have enough confidence in their management team to award them power of attorney over their business affairs. It is unfair for artists to insist that the manager or agent obtain their consent before making a deal.

6. *Never hog the spotlight.*   If you take the artist's public away even for a moment, the artist will resent you. It is the artist's show. You may be directing a puppet artist, but behind the puppet is an all-too-human psyche. Backstage, onstage, so long as the media and the artist's public are involved, your place is behind the artist, outside the photographer's rangefinder, and removed from the artist's idolizing (let's hope) fans.

88

Some Things
Cannot Be Controlled

Many vested interests are at loggerheads with the contemporary music agency. Some halls will not permit rock music; others, fearing excessive damage to the facility, charge unfair premium rates and insist on maximum security protection. Agents have no control over how many union stagehands and Teamsters will be assigned to an artist's production. Some halls, such as Madison Square Garden, require the concert promoter to pay for local union musicians regardless of whether they are needed for a rock concert (generally speaking, they never are). Factors such as these, coupled with the rising costs for heating fuel, utilities, labor, and facility upkeep—not agency greed—are the primary reasons ticket prices go up.

Managers have their own public relations battles to fight, but on different battlefields. The personal management profession has been under invasion in the last decade by record companies, independent record producers, concert promoters, and star-crazed outsiders. The image of what a personal manager should be has been grossly distorted. Quality personal managers, already the smallest group of industry professionals, are losing artists to big-name producers out for a quick killing. Greed seems to be in; long-term artist development, which only recently broke Billy Joel, Pablo Cruise, and Fleetwood Mac, is becoming more and more of an anomaly. The outlook, which is bleak, calls for bland music, loud noise, and violent theatrics. What this has to do with the art of music, I don't know.

It may already be too late for management and agency purists to alter the course of the Greed Machine. But the beginning manager's and agent's survival may depend on standing up to be counted among the exceptional few. These people will view their professions as highly specialized, full-time callings. They will be prepared to let the artist grow in his own time and in his own way. They will be high-stakes gamblers, but they will be music people before. they will be money collectors. This philosophy, I believe, is the right direction for managers and agents to take in the '80s and beyond.

PART 9

Concert Promotion Needs

A far more comprehensive study of concert promotion needs can be found in another book in the Zadoc Music Business Series, *Promoting Rock Concerts*, written by Howard Stein and myself and published by Schirmer Books.

89

How to Succeed as a Concert Promoter

Concert promotion is a service business. The services provided by a concert promoter includes the physical staging of a live concert event, exposing new artists, selling tickets, providing advertising and publicity, arranging for crowd control, and accounting for ticket sales after the concert. The reason there are concert promoters is because agents, artists, and managers don't want to bother handling the myriad details that surround a major concert production. The promoter's income is a small percentage—usually 10 to 20 percent—of the concert's gross income.

Years ago, when rock was just beginning to happen, a wave of enterprising young promoters competed for business with the major agencies. The best of these promoters— people like Bill Graham, Ron Delsener, Jim Rissmiller, Larry Magid, and Howard Stein—were given verbal exclusivities to work the agency's major acts. Medieval fiefdoms were chiseled out of the live concert domain, with one leading monopolistic promoter in each major U.S. city. The key to success in concert promotion is being able to present major attractions with guaranteed sell-out drawing power. The overriding problem facing aspiring concert promoters in the '80s is that many of the major monopolistic promoters from the '60s are still very much in control of their fiefdoms, and show no evidence of retiring.

In order to survive in the concert promotion business today, a new promoter must concentrate on being of immediate utilitarian value to a major agency. This translates into a specific course of action, which is (a) to find an open city where competition between promoters still goes on; (b) to find a facility that would be suitable for showcasing the agency's new acts; (c) to get permission from the facility manager to produce live concerts; (d) to start servicing the agent's new acts; and (e) to continue servicing the agency's new attractions until such time as the agency says, "You can come in from out of the cold now. We'll start giving you middle-level and major acts so that you can start making some money."

As can be seen from this stark scenario, concert promotion is the least desirable music business profession. It is a very unfair business that offers the promoter no tangible assets, security, or equity—only unceasing servitude to the agency for years, with a negative potential for deriving income from unknown acts. Unless you have a cast-iron stomach, nerves of steel, and a magic bullet for improving the odds, concert promotion probably isn't right for you as a career.

90

What to Say to the Agent

If, after reading the last section, you are still of a mind to proceed as a concert promoter, you will have to make contact with a number of major booking agencies. Here are five things to say in your first verbal exchange:

1. You are not a newcomer to concert promotion, but have been promoting shows for campus organizations, underground theatres, and friends.

2. You have lined up a 150- to 400-seat facility in a secondary or primary market. The facility is in a high-traffic area and caters to young people. The facility manager has agreed in principle to letting the promoter showcase concerts featuring the agency's newly signed unknown talent.

3. You want to establish your true value to the agency where it counts the most: by helping the agency break new talent. Your only request is that, in time, the agency will agree to let you promote its larger acts in larger facilities within your market area.

4. You understand that it is a cash-and-carry business, and that until your credit rating is established you may have to pay all your talent costs up front.

5. You will describe your role as a concert promoter to the agent. This role is to handle the logistics of advertising and producing concerts. You do not intend to steal acts from the manager or agent. You have no aspirations to become a record producer or music publisher. Your special interest is to promote concerts to the best of your ability and to become a favored promoter in the agency's concert distribution scheme.

Needless to say, promoters must have the experience, contacts, and cash to justify these statements. Their intentions must be genuine, too—i.e., if an agent gets a report from the manager that the promoter overstepped his bounds with an act, the agent will blacklist that promoter for life.

Even at the lowest level, it is very difficult today to wedge one's foot into the concert promotion industry. A major promoter's monopoly extends not only to the largest prime facilities in town, but the the smallest prime showcase venues for unknown talent. Once an unknown artist plays for an established promoter, it is almost impossible for a junior-level promoter to handle that act whenever it plays at that local market. Practically every city today has an equivalent to New York City's Bottom Line or L.A.'s Roxy. But if you want to be a concert promoter, you're going to have to find, somewhere in the United States, a hitherto overlooked, dynamite venue.

91

Coming to Grips with the No-deal Deal

Most promoters just getting started are under the misguided impression that promoters can wheel and deal for the price of talent. In reality, once an agent establishes a price for an act, it's take it or leave it. This policy applies to acts at every level in the business, including new acts.

At the lower end of the business, agents usually don't bother with deals based on a percentage of the gate. Promoters are asked to pay a flat fee, 50 percent up front and 50 percent on the day the act performs. As soon as an act gets big enough for the agent to sense significant profits, the deal becomes a guarantee-plus-percentage situation. This means that the promoter must pay the act a nonreturnable talent fee, regardless of how many seats are sold, plus, in the event that gross income after taxes exceeds total expenditures, a specified percentage of the overage, or net profit.

The pricing of middle-level and major concerts has been

reduced to a science. The agent and promoter both know how many seats there are in the facility, and how many seats will actually be put on sale. They will establish ticket prices together, and arrive at what is called the GP, or gross potential, for the concert. The agent and promoter both should know what the total costs against the GP will be for producing the event. Total costs include facility rent, ticket printing, advertising, internal and external security, box-office personnel, stagehands, Teamsters, rental of sound and light equipment, instrument rentals, tuning, transportation, meals and insurance. Using this precise information, the agent will decide how much of a PC or percentage, the act will take of the overage. Some acts will take a 50 percent PC; stronger acts will take a 75 or 85 percent PC. Giant events in outdoor stadiums may yield the promoter only 10 percent of the overage, PROVIDED THERE IS ONE. If there's not an overage, the promoter may not get paid. Everyone else will have been taken care of handsomely, but unless the event is a complete sellout the promoter may end up—and very often does—either with nothing or with a loss.

The only area left to negotiate in the concert promotion business is when, on a guarantee-plus-PC deal, the promoter can begin to earn some money. Promoters should try to get at least one-half of their percentage money immediately after break-even has been attained. That way, if the concert doesn't sell out 100 percent the act and the promoter will make less money, but at least the promoter will receive some compensation.

If, on the other hand, the promoter allows the act to take its PC cut first, and the concert was, say, only an 85 percent sellout, the promoter might get stuck holding the bag. Agents do not allow promoters to take all of the PC immediately after break-even, since they fear that promoters would lose their incentive to sell the concert out completely. But it is imperative for promoters to be able to negotiate as much of the PC immediately after break-even as possible.

Successful concert promoters must do a high volume of concerts every year to cancel out the inevitable non-revenue-producing events. Money earned is usually invested right back into the business in order to secure new concerts. Very few promoters can truthfully say that they made their millions in this capital-depleting, non-interest-bearing business.

92

Tips on Saving Money

It is very hard to save money as a concert promoter. Every act that is booked through a major talent agency makes demands upon the promoter that must be honored. If an act wants to use its own sound and light equipment, there's nothing to talk about, nothing to argue: if the promoter wants the act, the promoter must pay the price established by the agency for sound and lights. If an act wants five cases of imported beer, the promoter cannot substitute a cheaper American beer. If the act walks into its dressing room and finds only three cases of imported beer instead of five cases, the act may refuse to go through with the concert. Whatever the act wants—no matter how unreasonable the demands may seem—the promoter must provide it.

Within these almost unbearable constraints, there are ingenious ways for saving dollars and cents that, over the course of a year, may aggregate into substantial savings. Here are some of those ways.

1. Newspaper and radio advertising.   If you are planning to do a substantial amount of newspaper and radio advertising, you should be able to obtain reduced per-line or per-commercial rates. The step beyond this is to invite the leading rock station in town to exchange no-cost inclusion of the station's call letters in the promoter's newspaper ads for a special favored-nations spot commercial rate for thirty- and sixty-second spots. In one market that I am personally familiar with, the normal price of a sixty-second spot is $200; the same spot costs the favored-nations promoter $40.

Another real money saver is to use one-column strip ads in newspapers rather than individual display ads for each event. A long, single-column strip ad has the depth to command the reader's attention, but at a fraction of the cost of a half-dozen separate two- or three-column display ads.

2. Stagehands.   Try not to let the stagehands union ride roughshod over you. When a concert is in the planning stage, go over the particulars with the head of the stagehands union. Tell this person, "I have the act's concert rider in front of me, and it says that the act's road crew consists of fifteen able-bodied men. Between load-in time and the sound check, we're going to have to install a three-ton lighting truss, fly twenty speakers from the ceiling, position ten amplifiers onstage, and mount a thirty-five-foot-high backdrop. How many men is it going to take?" Once the union chief has committed to a specific number of stagehands, you're in good shape to hold that person to his word.

3. Insurance premiums.   Many different types of insurance, from bodily injury to stick-up insurance, have a bearing on the concert promotion business. If you're planning to do a lot of concerts, the insurance company should be able to offer you a package deal. Each concert will have a proportionally lower insurance cost than if you were to go to the insurance broker on a concert-by-concert basis.

4. Limousines.   Many acts, after playing a successful gig and partying, elect to cruise around the city all night in their chauffeur-driven limousines. This should not be done, however, at the promoter's expense. Any use of limousines beyond basic transportation to and from the airport, the hotel, and the concert facility should be borne by the act, not the promoter.

5. *Damages.*   After a big concert, there are bound to be some damaged chairs, broken lighting fixtures, and plumbing problems caused by the promoter's audience. Estimated damages should be walked off immediately after the concert in a joint inspection by the promoter and the facility manager. Never allow a facility to estimate damage expenses on its own.

6. *Tour support.*   Most major labels are heavily involved today in subsidizing concert appearances by their acts. Record companies may help pay for radio commercials and newspaper ads; they may also buy large blocks of seats for their employees. Next to the agent, the director of tour support at the record company may be the most important person for a promoter to have in his corner.

7. *Overtime.*   This is the bane of all concert promoters. The doors of the concert facility must open to the public on time. The act has to complete its set, including encores, on time. Every dollar of overtime expense is a dollar taken away from the concert promoter's income.

93

Be Ready for Emergencies on the Day of the Concert

Every experienced promoter has stories to tell about the sound truck that never made it to the concert, the costume van that was stolen, or the piano company that accidentally rented the right instrument to the wrong customer. Protect yourself from these and other potential hazards by planning in depth, well in advance of the show. Promoters should be able to rely on at least one backup caterer, limousine service, sound and light supplier, portable stage company, and spare electrician. A list of key personnel, including the facility manager, union stewards, road manager, box-office treasurer, medical doctor, city police chief, head of in-house security, electrician, and caterer, along with telephone numbers where these people can be reached at any hour on the day of the show, is another sensible precaution.

Arrive early at the facility on the day of the concert, and don't leave to have lunch. Don't leave for anything. Make sure things are going smoothly, and that the doors of the facility will open to the public on time.

During the load-in, allow the road manager to make command decisions on the deployment of the production labor force. The promoter may know his facility inside and out, but the road manager knows how long it takes to assemble the act's lighting truss, stage backdrop, sound system, mixing platform, and onstage props. Practically speaking, the concert promoter's boss throughout the show—up to and including the reconciliation of sold and unsold tickets in the box office—is the act's road manager.

Promoters, however, can't be everywhere at once. On the day of the concert, the promoter will employ a production coordinator to oversee the load-in of equipment, and perhaps a stage manager, who will be available to handle any problems involving the union stagehands, the artist's road crew, Teamsters, and other personnel working onstage or backstage.

94

Choose Your Agency Carefully

Concert promoters are in intense competition with each other, but so are agencies. The naive tendency is for promoters to make their decisions exclusively in terms of the artist, but in reality I think it's more important to make decisions based on the strength of a particular agency and to what extent they're willing to play ball. It is better to anticipate making enemies (almost certainly you will) and make a pact with the strongest one-stop agency than to rely on playing the field.

Agents may appear to be the villains in the concert promotion business, but there's no way to get ahead as a major promoter without them. Especially at the beginning, promoters should not risk talking directly with either the act or the act's manager. Negotiation has to proceed through the agency. Everything must go through channels until the promoter is advised otherwise.

Many people with excellent promotional instincts are taking a hard look today at other opportunities involving music and live audiences. Disco clubs such as Studio 54 and Xenon in New York City can be used for a variety of purposes, including dancing, concerts, and parties. Income is derived not only from selling tickets and annual memberships, but also from food, beverages, and photographic sessions. The added advantage of a disco club is that the music being promoted is on record. The often outrageous demands of artists, agents, and managers can, with a disco, be sidestepped completely.

PART 10

Publicity Needs

95

If the Story Isn't Newsworthy, It Will Never Make It

The trick to getting publicity is not to hire an expensive public relations firm (Note: One thing all publicists do is charge a fortune—they are the single most overpriced element in the music business). The trick is to do something that the media considers truly newsworthy. If what you're doing will help sell papers and boost ratings, you will eventually get publicity; if what you're doing is not considered newsworthy, you will be frustrated in your attempts to get publicity, whether or not you hire a professional public relations firm. I have yet to meet a PR specialist who has been willing to concede this fundamental point.

The primary reason that public relations firms exist is not because they are better story creators than the managers, agents, promoters, artists, and marketing professionals who hire them. The primary reason is that most PR clients can't be bothered with the onerous job of hounding editors for stories. Major celebrities sell papers, not the unknown artist just signed to his first recording contract. The rise from obscurity to concert reviews, mini-profiles, feature stories, radio interviews, feature cover stories, and prime-time TV interviews can take years of brute physical labor.

Getting publicity is definitely a chore, yet it also has to be handled with a sense of taste and timing. If the story is handled ineptly or sold too hard, it will go down the tubes. Thus the PR specialist argues, "Let me handle this assignment. I know the people at the newspapers and stations very well. We see each other all the time. We talk on the telephone all the time. If anyone can sell this story, it's me."

That may be true. It is equally true that no professional newspaper editor or program director of a station will risk his own neck—not to mention the circulation of the paper or the ratings of the station—by publicizing a story whose newsworthiness is at all suspect. The question potential PR clients should ask is, "How long will I have to pay my publicist between $250 and $500 a month in order to see results? Is my career truly on the verge of taking off, or will it be another three years before I'm ready to wrest a cover photo away from Mick Jagger?"

An even more basic question would be, "Is PR really worth it?" Certainly PR can be extremely valuable. It can save the client a great deal of money that would otherwise have to be allocated for advertising. But publicity only makes sense if the timing is right. If it comes before the artist is seasoned, it may take the form of disadvantageous, negative criticism. If it comes too late, the artist may already have decided to change from one music business career to another, or quit the profession altogether.

I personally think that the importance of PR for unattached newcomers is vastly overrated. The logical way to proceed, in my opinion, is to do first things first. First you need exposure. First you have to get your act together. First you need an excellent management team. When multiple story requests start coming in, then you will need an outside assist from a PR professional. Until then, be grateful that the media are allowing your mistakes to go unrecorded.

96

Handling Publicity for a New Organization

The best way for beginners to handle publicity is to do it themselves. So long as somebody in the group's retinue has the ability to write decently, the group should save money and prepare, print, and distribute its own fundamental PR tool, the press release.

Press releases should be short, punchy, typed, and easy to read. The story should be told in three or four paragraphs; a title for the story should be centered in a box at the top of the page. Name the principal players in the group, where the group is playing and with whom the group is affiliated (e.g., record company, producer, publisher, manager, agent). At the bottom of the press release give a telephone number for the group spokesperson to be contacted for additional information. This last suggestion, while it is a good habit to get into, does not imply that reporters actually call unknown groups. Until such time as the group attains superstardom (and let's hope it does), the PR spokesperson must always take the initiative with follow-through phone calls.

The PR spokesperson should be highly articulate on the telephone, with excellent antennae for gauging whether the reporter on the other end is interested. Knowing whom to call does not require purchasing an expensive list of media contacts. All that is needed is for the PR spokesperson to dial each major newspaper, magazine, and radio and TV station in town, get the names and addresses of the entertainment or music editors, and retain this list for future reference.

If it's hard to get a story in a particular newspaper or magazine, that's where you want to be. The more resistance, the larger the circulation. Stories are much easier to obtain in the music business trades, but their value to the group may be inconsequential. In my experience, if the paper, radio, or TV station doesn't have a very large audience, it's not worth going after for publicity.

Start with the major papers in town. Most music stories can be pitched in a variety of ways, as either pure music, human interest, education, careers, or life styles pieces. Work systematically for one or two hours at the most, but never stop plugging. You job is not only to sell stories, but to sell the group's dedication to succeed. Over the years, as you return again and again to the same media contacts, the manner in which you are perceived as a person will have a significant impact on whether the group gets publicity. In other words, it pays to be nice.

Always invite members of the press to be your guests at a concert. Members of the press should never be asked to pay admission, although some may insist on paying their own way and paying for their meals. It goes without saying that members of the press should also receive free promotional copies of records, tapes, and sheet music.

97

Tips on Getting Publicity

•

Here are five problem-solving suggestions for dealing with newspapers, magazines, and radio and TV stations:

1. Don't talk to more than one reporter at a time on the paper about your story.   Find out who the most likely reporter would be to cover your story, but then keep the conversation on a confidential basis until the reporter decides what to do. If the right reporter is out to lunch or not at his desk, wait for him to return. It is very unprofessional to offer three, four or five reporters on the same paper the same story.

2. Honor exclusivity requests.   Very often the only way you can get a reporter to do a story is if it's on an exclusive basis—i.e., no other paper in town will be able to do a similar piece. If that's the way it's got to be, first decide whether it's in your best interest to stop pitching the story to other publications. If you decide to give the reporter an exclusive, you should immediately stop calling other reporters with that particular story angle. If you have already approached other papers, be honest with the reporter who wants the exclusive, tell him that you approached the other papers, but that you will not follow up with them. Members of the press can get quite nasty with news sources who don't honor exclusivity commitments.

3. *Try to get a photograph wherever possible.*   Pictures do make an important difference to readers. Always ask if the paper or magazine wants a photo. Pictures should be 8x10 black and white glossies, preferably action photographs that fit the story, with the name, address, and telephone number of the PR spokesperson on the reverse side.

4. *Ask permission to read the story prior to publication.* The *New York Times* won't allow you to do this. Neither will *Time, Newsweek,* or the *Los Angeles Times.* But it never hurts to ask underground papers or trade magazines whether it is possible to look over a story for typographical errors and historical accuracy prior to publication. So many times what appears in print is either slightly or grossly incorrect. Don't expect $50-a-week stringers to write as well or as carefully as salaried full-time professionals. Every subject of a newspaper or magazine article has a right to be concerned about how the story actually reads, so by all means ask. The next worst thing that can happen is for a paper to say no. The worst thing that can happen, of course, is for the story to run with distorted information that damages your career.

5. *Always be a professional with a reporter.*   Don't try to get too friendly with members of the press. Most reporters take themselves and their profession quite seriously. They prefer keeping a professional distance. Coming on too strong with some reporters may literally frighten them away.

98

How to Talk to Reporters

Just be yourself—that's the most important thing. Be straightforward, stick to the story, and be careful that you don't badmouth anyone. Not even stars can afford to take chances with the press.

It's always better to sound up rather than down. Nobody wants to hear your sob story. Reporters want to know what you're doing that's exciting, that's captivating to people, that's responsible for your being in the same room with this delegate from the newspaper or magazine.

If you get to do radio or TV interviews, make your answers very short. Remember that it's not your show. The air personality has to feel that he had a good balance of time with you, as well as an excellent rapport. Never try to make an air personality look foolish.

Publicity is a very forward-moving kind of activity. In order for your career to develop, the story or interview you grant today must lead to some future story or interview. Do have consideration for the person asking questions, and show your appreciation by writing thank-you notes (much better, in this instance, than calling to say thanks). Don't be late for appointments with the press when you're starting up. One other thing: never lie to a reporter.

If you want to succeed in the music business, you'll have to acknowledge the power of good public relations and learn how to master it.

SUMMATION

Forging Ahead

The battle for music business survival goes on. Every day, thousands of people decide to get into the business. Every night, thousands more grit their teeth and decide to stay in the business. Infrequently, a handful of lucky, talented individuals emerge not only as survivors, but stars of the industry. I am sure the odds against this happening in the United States today are greater than one chance in 10,000. But whatever the odds, if you, the reader, wish to pursue a career in the music business, there's only one thing to do: forge ahead.

This book is setting a new course for how to make it. In a short phrase, I'd summarize it as the commonsense approach. Supporters of the commonsense approach will think before they take action. They will start by taking a very good look at themselves and what they want to be. They will develop a specific business plan with attainable goals.

They will call the right people, and offer to become associated with these people in the right way. They will be team members, not stars. They will have no delusions about their true value, as beginners, to the music industry. They will take whatever they can get at the start. Once in, they will apply themselves as never before to improving their art, finding the best possible management team, and graduating to the next higher success plateau.

Nothing worth doing in life is easy. But as a music business educator, I am appalled at the number of students who seem hell-bent on making it harder to get ahead rather than easier. If you are such a person, I would plead with you to please, for your own sake, wake up. Wake up to the importance of being commonsensical about a career in the music business. It is a business first, an art medium second. It is a money-hungry business, not a charitable, public-spirited business. It is a business peopled by brilliant, brash, creative, egomaniacal, cloddish, and moronic individuals: they may all look alike, they may all act alike, but if you don't learn how to choose the winners from the losers, your music business enterprise is doomed. It is a business that has established minimum performance standards in every conceivable job category. Generally speaking, the minimum performance standard today, in all fields, is excellence.

Patience, perhaps, is the supreme virtue of the battler for music business survival. Being patient is the supreme test of one's dedication to succeed. Patience is also the most effective weapon in the beginning combatant's arsenal for defending against the pink-slip, letdown feeling. Learning to wait for the right time to present a song or artist demo, or to make a telephone call requesting a job, is very, very important.

Otherwise, I have found that 99 percent of being able to do anything well depends on confidence. You must feel on top of the world. The only people you can afford being in business with are people who make you feel confident. Patience breeds confidence; confidence breeds success. The trick is to temper being patient and having confidence with the realities of the music business. That's why this book was assembled.

This seems an appropriate time (certainly I've been patient!) to wish each of my readers the best of luck in their personal battle for success in the music business. All of you will need it. Some of you may actually make it, though not as many as I'd like. As for the people who don't make it, it may actually be the best thing that ever happened to you. I can't tell you how many people I know—including myself—who started out wanting to be a musician, but changed. It's far more important to come to grips with who you are and what your talents suit you for than to throw your life away because you didn't become a recording artist.

The music business is a whacky, often thankless, essentially unbusinesslike business where gut instinct and luck still prevail. If you can begin applying the commonsense approach to what, in my opinion, really counts—being happy, making a decent living, and having a place to come home to every night—you may end up being more envied than envious.